Strategy Toolbox

Strategy Toolbox

50 Models to Foster Strategic Dialogue

Simon Reese

BUSINESS EXPERT PRESS

Leader in applied, concise business books

Strategy Toolbox: 50 Models to Foster Strategic Dialogue

Cover design by Charlene Kronstedt

Interior design by S4Carlisle Publishing Services, Chennai, India

First published in 2025 by
Business Expert Press, LLC
222 East 46th Street, New York, NY 10017
www.businessexpertpress.com

ISBN-13: 978-1-63742-840-5 (paperback)
ISBN-13: 978-1-63742-841-2 (e-book)

Business Expert Press Strategic Management Collection

First edition: 2025

10 9 8 7 6 5 4 3 2 1

EU SAFETY REPRESENTATIVE
Mare Nostrum Group B.V.
Mauritskade 21D
1091 GC Amsterdam
The Netherlands
gpsr@mare-nostrum.co.uk

Description

Strategy Toolbox **proves that strategy doesn't need to be tough—armed with the right tools, you can foster meaningful dialogue and clear direction, turning complexity into actionable results.**

In the world of business strategy, the key to success lies not just in having the right answers but in asking the right questions—and fostering meaningful dialogue along the way. *Strategy Toolbox* transforms the daunting task of strategy design into a structured and collaborative process, combining the 5 Is Model (Information, Issues, Insights, Implications, Implementation) with the 6 Cs framework (Company, Characteristics, Customers, Competitors, Climate, Consolidation). Together, these frameworks help teams turn complexity into clarity and actionable results.

The book is methodically organized into six sections, each exploring a distinct element of strategy through eight essential tools. At the end of each section, concise summaries and checklists simplify the process, ensuring teams stay aligned and focused as they move through the stages of analysis and design in their quest to answer strategic questions.

Created for both MBA students and business professionals, *Strategy Toolbox* equips readers with a clear roadmap for tackling real-world strategic challenges. By viewing strategic models as starting points for dialogue, this book empowers teams to collaboratively uncover insights, align on priorities by understanding implications, and craft implementable strategies that drive impactful outcomes.

Contents

List of Models .... *xi*

Introduction .... *xiii*

          Navigating the Sea of Information: The 5 Is Model xiii

          Diving into This Book xv

          Traversing the Pages xv

          Mapping Your Journey: The 6 Cs model xv

          Understanding Your Compass: The Power

              and Perils of Models xvii

Section 1   Company: Our Most Factual Knowledge

              Within Our Control 1

          Resource-Based View (RBV) of Strategy 2

          Porter's Value Chain Analysis 6

          VRIO Analysis 11

          Kay's Distinctive Capabilities Framework 15

          SWOT Analysis 19

          TOWS Analysis 22

          SOAR Analysis 26

          Company Checklist 30

Section 2   Characteristics: Still Factual and Controllable 31

          Kotler's 5 Product Levels 33

          Diffusion of Innovation 37

          Product Life Cycle Stages 41

          Break-Even Analysis 45

          Pareto Analysis 48

          BCG Growth-Share Matrix 52

          McKinsey's Three Horizons of Growth 56

          Characteristic Checklist 60

Section 3   Customers and Collaborators: Increasing
             Inferential Knowledge with Less Control 61
             Jobs-to-Be-Done (Outcome-Driven Innovation) 63
             Hierarchy of Needs (Value Pyramid) 66
             Value Proposition Canvas 71
             4 Cs of Inter-company Collaboration 75
             Segment–Target–Position (STP)....................................80
             Customer Lifetime Value 84
             The Value Stick...88
             Customer and Collaborator Checklist............................94
Section 4   Competitors: Inferential with Almost No Control........97
             HHI Index (Competitive Concentration)......................99
             Rule of Three and Four...103
             Porter's Four Corners..106
             Competitor Profile Matrix 111
             Strategic Group Analysis...115
             Red Queen Effect 120
             Co-opetition..124
             Competitor Checklist...129
Section 5   Climate: Inferential and Uncontrollable 131
             CAGE Analysis..132
             PESTEL 137
             Porter's Diamond of National Advantage....................140
             Porter's Five Forces 144
             Industry Profit Pools or Industry Value
                 Chain Analysis 149
             Industry Life Cycle Stages...152
             ADL Matrix 158
             Climate Checklist..162
Section 6   Consolidation: Pulling Everything Together 165
             SPACE Analysis...168
             Attack and Defense Strategy Plan 173
             Lafley and Martin's 5-Step Strategy Model.................179
             Mintzberg's 5 Ps of Strategy.......................................183
             Ohmae's 3 Cs Model 187

Porter's Generic Strategies..191
Hambrick and Fredrickson's Strategy Diamond............196
The Emergent Approach to Strategy 200

Concluding Thoughts 207
About the Author..209
Endnotes 211
Index 215

List of Models

Model 1 of 50: The 5 Is xiv

Model 2 of 50: The 6 Cs xvi

Model 3 of 50: The Resource-Based View Diagnosis 3

Model 4 of 50: Value Chain Dissection 7

Model 5 of 50: The VRIO Flow Chart 11

Model 6 of 50: The Distinctive Capabilities Table 16

Model 7 of 50: The SWOT Table 19

Model 8 of 50: The SWOT to TOWS Linkage 23

Model 9 of 50: The SOAR Matrix 26

Model 10 of 50: Company Assessment Team Checklist 30

Model 11 of 50: 5 Product Levels 33

Model 12 of 50: Diffusion of Innovation 37

Model 13 of 50: Product Life Cycle 41

Model 14 of 50: Break-Even Analysis 45

Model 15 of 50: Pareto Analysis 49

Model 16 of 50: BCG Growth-Share Table 52

Model 17 of 50: McKinsey's Three Horizons of Growth Table 56

Model 18 of 50: Characteristics Checklist 60

Model 19 of 50: Jobs-to-Be-Done Table 63

Model 20 of 50: Customer Hierarchy of Needs 67

Model 21 of 50: Value Proposition Canvas 71

Model 22 of 50: Reese's 4 Cs of Inter-company Collaboration 75

Model 23 of 50: Segment–Target–Position (STP) Model 80

Model 24 of 50: Customer Lifetime Value 84

Model 25 of 50: Value Stick 89

Model 26 of 50: Customer and Collaborator Checklist 95

Model 27 of 50: HHI Index 99

Model 28 of 50: Rules of Three and Four 103

Model 29 of 50: Porter's Four Corners 107

Model 30 of 50: Competitive Profile Matrix 112

Model 31 of 50: Strategic Group Analysis 116

Model 32 of 50: Red Queen Effect...121

Model 33 of 50: Co-opetition Matrix...125

Model 34 of 50: Competitor Checklist...130

Model 35 of 50: CAGE Model..133

Model 36 of 50: PESTEL...137

Model 37 of 50: Porter's Diamond of National Advantage 141

Model 38 of 50: Porter's Five Forces...145

Model 39 of 50: Industry Profit Pools 149

Model 40 of 50: Industry Life Cycle Stages 153

Model 41 of 50: ADL Matrix..158

Model 42 of 50: Climate Checklist 163

Model 43 of 50: SPACE Analysis 168

Model 44 of 50: Attack and Defense Strategy...................................174

Model 45 of 50: 5-Step Strategy Model...180

Model 46 of 50: 5 Ps of Strategy..183

Model 47 of 50: 3 Cs Model 187

Model 48 of 50: Porter's Generic Strategies 192

Model 49 of 50: Strategy Diamond 196

Model 50 of 50: The Emergent Strategy Approach 201

Introduction

Navigating the Sea of Information: The 5 Is Model

In the ever-evolving world of business strategy, where an overwhelming amount of data can seem like an endless ocean, students and strategists face a common challenge when confronted with a strategic question: transforming information quickly and effectively into actionable insights that lead to clear, implementable strategies. With over two decades of experience as a corporate strategist and MBA-level instructor, I recognized a crucial gap in the journey from data to action. Too often, we get stuck—overwhelmed by information and issues—without the ability to accelerate toward actionable insights and effective strategy.

This realization led me to create the 5 Is model, a simple yet powerful framework designed to clarify and guide this process. Inspired by Seth Godin's book *Linchpin* and his concept of the "law of linchpin leverage," I found parallels to the 5 Is model. While not identical, Godin's law captures a similar idea: to reach the point of creating the greatest value with the least effort. The 5 Is model builds on this insight to provide a structured pathway.

My MBA students and my team at work often lose themselves in "information and issues" mode. They dive into countless articles, competitor assessments, and industry research, becoming data gatherers rather than insight creators. Occasionally, they take it further, identifying issues hidden in the information—often caused by gaps in data sources or emerging trends. While this analysis is commendable, it's time-consuming and is increasingly less valuable as AI technology improves.

The 5 Is model highlights the crucial next step: creating insights—the inflection point where real value emerges. Insights go beyond identifying issues; they extract the "so what" from an issue, transforming it into a critical value point. I encourage my students and colleagues alike to aim for insights swiftly. Don't drown your audience in data or bog them down with all the issues you uncovered; focus instead on the key takeaway—the "so what."

But the 5 Is don't end with insights. The following steps amplify the value even further, where you stand out as a student or strategist. After forming insights, connect them to your context, whether it's your organization or a case study. This step, called Implications, demonstrates how insights impact your situation. If the insight is important, the implications are often significant.

Finally, move on to action—decide what to do next and implement the strategy with an eye toward measurable impact. Few make it to this ultimate step, but all should aspire to reach it as quickly and effectively as possible.

Model 1 of 50: The 5 Is

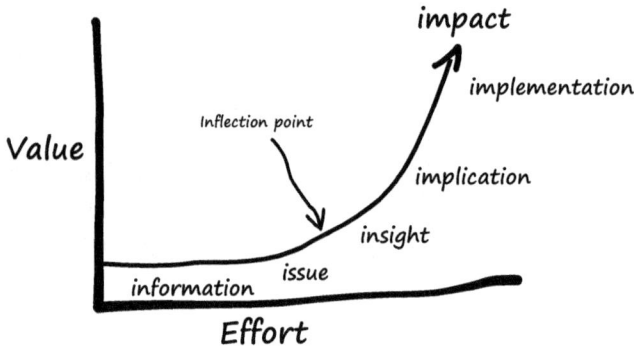

The effectiveness of the 5 Is model in academic and professional settings inspired me to reflect on our existing tools and frameworks. What models were we using to help students quickly progress through the 5 Is?

This book was born out of that reflection. It explores combining select strategy models to help you and your team move through the 5 Is more easily. The premise is simple: once you have your strategic question (be it a case analysis question in class or a question about your business) organize strategic models into cohesive groups to streamline information transformation and guide you and your team toward implementable, impactful strategies.

Whether you're a new strategy student or a seasoned professional, this book provides a practical guide to essential strategy models. Join me on this journey to apply strategic models and create a more direct path through the information landscape—from identifying issues to forming insights, assessing implications, and implementing solutions.

Diving into This Book

In the complex landscape of business strategy, even when the strategic question is clear you may find yourself overwhelmed by information, unsure of which issues matter most, or struggling to turn information into an actionable plan. This book is here to help. Designed as a quick-reference toolbox for both classroom learning and corporate practice, it distills essential models for practical application without overwhelming you with details. Think of this book as your personal toolkit for navigating each step of the 5 Is process.

Traversing the Pages

This book begins with the model summaries I've developed for my MBA students over the years. These concise references clarify when and how to use each model. Some models include minor adaptations I've found helpful for making them easier to apply. Illustrations are included to aid understanding, organize information, and help you get started. As I often tell my students, these models aren't confined to case analysis in class; they're tools you can carry into the corporate world for structuring information, developing insights, and creating implementable strategies.

As you review this toolbox, explore each model's historical background, example contexts, practical steps, and illustrations just as I would draw them on the whiteboard. Your objective is to evaluate each model's applicability to your strategic questions and take insightful notes as you work through the steps. Keep this toolbox close as you tackle strategic questions, turning it into your personal resource for strategy development.

Mapping Your Journey: The 6 Cs model

This toolbox is structured into six sections around the 6 Cs—Company, Characteristics, Customers, Competitors, Climate, and Consolidation—and provides a comprehensive strategic analysis and decision-making framework. Each model within a category offers methods corresponding to the specific business aspect represented by its "C." This 6 Cs framework also loosely aligns with Kenichi Ohmae's 3 Cs model from *The Mind of the Strategist*, which focuses on the Company, Customers, and Competitors. By expanding to six categories, the situational analysis is more structured.

The 6 Cs are flexible and versatile; they offer a framework for selecting models that align with multiple Cs based on your strategic questions. Imagine the 6 Cs as concentric circles: the inner circles represent areas where you have more organizational control and factual data, while the outer circles reflect less control and more inferential information.

The Company and Characteristics Cs focus on internal factors within your control, while Customers, Competitors, and Climate address external influences. Consolidation acts as a final stage, bringing the prior 5 Cs together. Within each category, models provide insights and action steps relevant to different strategic questions, making it easier to conduct a complete strategic analysis and make informed decisions.

Use the 6 Cs to map your journey by choosing the "C" most relevant to your strategic question. Then, refer to the final model in each section for a handy checklist to help your team assess that C.

Model 2 of 50: The 6 Cs

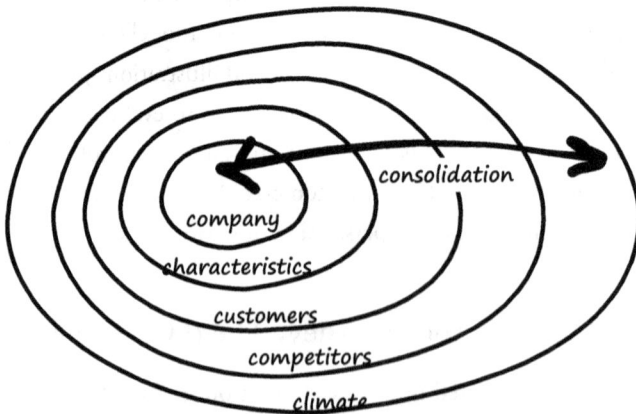

Understanding Your Compass: The Power and Perils of Models

In the flood of data and complexity, seeking structure and clarity is natural. Models serve as navigational aids that break down complex situations into manageable parts, allowing you to focus on essentials and make better decisions.

Think of the models in this toolbox as your compass—guiding your focus in the swirling sea of information. These models simplify data and enhance clarity of the ideas, breathing life into issues, insights, and implications. But as with any compass, understanding its limits is essential.

Using models brings benefits and potential biases. If you don't fully understand a tool, it may inadvertently filter out important information or create biases that distort your view. To maximize the strategic toolbox, view these models as dynamic frameworks—tools to debate, adjust, and adapt with your team.

Consider models as flexible guides for organizing thoughts, sparking discussions, and articulating ideas. Each model's real test comes when it meets real-world situations. Models are guides, not absolute truths—they need to be tested against reality to uncover biases and refine your approach.

Remember, the model itself is just a starting point; its true power lies in the conversations it generates. Without discussion, a model is like a compass without a map. Approach each model as a catalyst for strategic thinking that fuels valuable discussions in both academic and professional settings. Through these discussions, the real power of models comes to life, guiding us through the complexities of strategy with precision and insight.

SECTION 1

Company: Our Most Factual Knowledge Within Our Control

Assess your strengths, weaknesses, and organizational dynamics versus strategy.

The "Company" band serves as a realm for reflective assessment. Models in this section offer insights into your company, addressing questions such as its capabilities, strengths, weaknesses, competitive advantages, opportunities, and threats. This "C" provides a space where you exert the most control and possess factual knowledge, facilitating a deeper understanding of dynamics and interconnections.

Each model in this "C" offers a way to distill information about your company into actionable strategic moves. The section starts with the most internal view of the company's resources and value chain, then links those to competitive advantages to understand strengths and weaknesses. Once the internal view is understood, future opportunities and threats are overlaid to determine strategic resilience. As with all sections, this section concludes with a checklist tool to help facilitate group discussion about the Company.

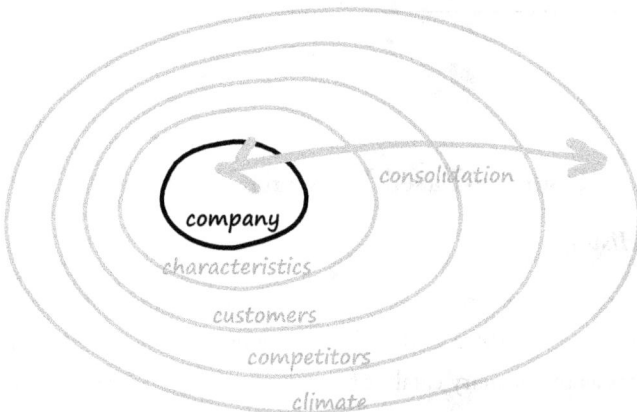

Quick exercise with your team:

Start your company assessment by conducting either leadership interviews or a leadership workshop. Ask a few simple questions to understand your organization's starting point. If you are conducting interviews, just ask the questions. If you are conducting a workshop, ask participants to write down their ideas or responses on individual slips of paper (or Post-it Notes).

Questions:
- *What is our competitive advantage?*
- *How is our competitive advantage sustainable?*
- *How are we organized around our competitive advantage?*
- *What opportunities exist to leverage our competitive advantage?*
- *What are the threats to our competitive advantage?*
- *How are we prepared to mitigate these threats?*

Categorize the sticky notes (or interview responses) and analyze them. Do you have alignment? Do you see a lack of clarity? The tools within Section 1 will help you better understand your company through the lens of the questions above. You'll notice these same questions in the final model of Section 1.

Resource-Based View (RBV) of Strategy

Brief History

The origins of the Resource-Based View (RBV) theory can be traced back to Edith Penrose's 1959 study, where she identified untapped managerial resources as the primary catalyst for growth.[1] Birger Wernerfelt provided an analysis of the concept in his article "A Resource-Based View of the Firm."[2] Further solidifying this theory, Jay Barney's 1991 article, "Firm Resources and Sustained Competitive Advantage," established a practical resource-based framework in the business domain.[3]

Model 3 of 50: The Resource-Based View Diagnosis

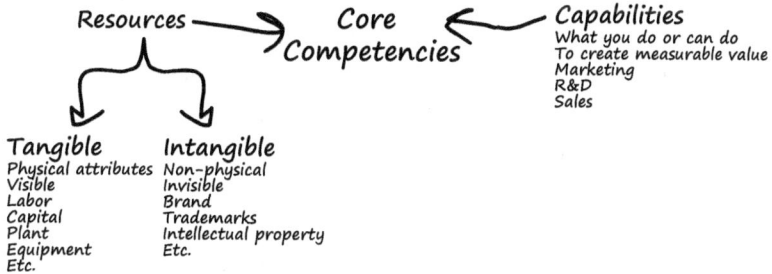

Resources ⟶ Core Competencies ⟵ Capabilities
What you do or can do
To create measurable value
Marketing
R&D
Sales

Tangible
Physical attributes
Visible
Labor
Capital
Plant
Equipment
Etc.

Intangible
Non-physical
Invisible
Brand
Trademarks
Intellectual property
Etc.

When to Use—Identify the Valuable Elements of Your Business

RBV aids in understanding the core competencies of your business. These unique strengths are embedded deeply within the organization. RBV provides a method to categorize resources, capabilities, and competencies. Penrose highlighted internal managerial resources' dual role as drivers and constraints on a firm's expansion. Wernerfelt analyzes and proposes strategic options tied to resources. Barney described the effective resource-based framework as a competitive advantage in the business domain. RBV aids in identifying the valuable elements comprising a business.

Context and Scenario for Use

The RBV theory is a strategic management framework that analyzes and leverages an organization's internal resources and capabilities to gain sustainable competitive advantage. Here are some scenarios where RBV theory can be effectively utilized:

- **Strategic Planning and Formulation:** Organizations often need to assess their resource base to determine their competitive positioning when developing strategies. The RBV theory helps in this process by guiding organizations in identifying and evaluating their tangible and intangible resources, such as physical assets, human capital, technology, brand reputation, and organizational culture. By thoroughly analyzing these resources, organizations can identify their core competencies and distinctive capabilities that set them apart from competitors.

- **Merger and Acquisition (M&A) Activities:** When considering acquiring or merging with another company, organizations must assess the target company's resources and capabilities to determine its potential for creating value. RBV theory provides a framework for evaluating the compatibility and complementarity of resources between the acquiring and target companies. This assessment helps identify potential synergies and risks associated with the M&A transaction, guiding decision-making and integration strategies.

- **Innovation and Organizational Renewal:** To remain competitive, organizations must adapt to changing market conditions and technological advancements. By leveraging their unique resources and capabilities, organizations can innovate and develop new products, services, or processes that create value for customers and differentiate them from competitors. The RBV theory encourages organizations to continuously invest in and develop their key resources to sustain their competitive advantage.

- **Competitive Positioning:** Organizations can use RBV to identify and focus on their unique strengths in highly competitive markets. Companies can develop strategies that enhance their market position and protect against competitive threats.

- **Resource Allocation:** Organizations can use RBV theory to make informed decisions about where to allocate resources for maximum impact. By identifying which resources contribute most to competitive advantage, companies can prioritize investments that strengthen these areas and improve overall performance.

- **Strategic Alliances and Partnerships:** When forming strategic alliances or partnerships, organizations can use RBV to assess the resources and capabilities of potential partners. This helps ensure that the partnership creates mutual value and enhances both parties' competitive positions.

RBV theory is applicable in various strategic management contexts where organizations aim to understand, leverage, and enhance their internal resources and capabilities to achieve sustainable competitive advantage. Whether in strategic planning, M&A activities, innovation initiatives, competitive positioning, resource allocation, or forming strategic alliances, the RBV theory provides valuable insights and guidance for organizational decision-making and strategic direction.

How to Use

In the RBV, a firm is seen as a distinctive amalgamation of resources and capabilities that create core competencies. Resources are broadly categorized into two main types: Tangible and Intangible. Tangible resources possess physical and observable attributes, while intangible resources lack physical attributes and remain invisible. Steps to using the RBV include:

1. Strategically group the resources that your organization relies upon into tangible and intangible.
2. Catalog the company's capabilities, encompassing organizational and managerial skills to coordinate diverse resources strategically. Capabilities, being intangible, play a crucial role in the RBV framework but are elusive.
3. Identify the core competencies. These are distinctive strengths deeply ingrained within a firm, enabling it to differentiate its products and services from competitors.

4. Determine if core competencies are fortified through strategic activities, creating a sustainable competitive advantage. Look for the orchestrating and reinforcing activities to understand the fully integrated system.

Outlining the RBV elements helps understand the distinctive aspects of the organization that create advantage and those that do not. RBV helps focus strategy across the integrated system to determine where to place effort and where not to.

Notes for Your Use

- **Gather Information:** Initiate by delving into your company's assets, structure, routines, and culture.
- **List and Sort:** Systematically categorize your resources into tangible and intangible groups while outlining capabilities.
- **Evaluate Alignment:** Scrutinize the reinforcement of your resources and the orchestration of your capabilities. Identify alignment and misalignment.
- **Compare and Integrate:** Compare your RBV with SWOT, SOAR, and Porter's Value Chain Analysis. Did you capture all essential elements?
- **Ensure Alignment:** Verify if your company's activities align with core competencies. Rectify any misalignment.
- **Implement Strategy:** Execute targeted actions to refine misalignment and sharpen focus across the integrated system.

Porter's Value Chain Analysis

Brief History

Michael Porter introduced the Value Chain Analysis in 1985 as a strategic tool outlined in his book *Competitive Advantage*.[4,5] This business management framework aids in identifying activities within an organization that contribute value to customers and those that do not.

Model 4 of 50: Value Chain Dissection

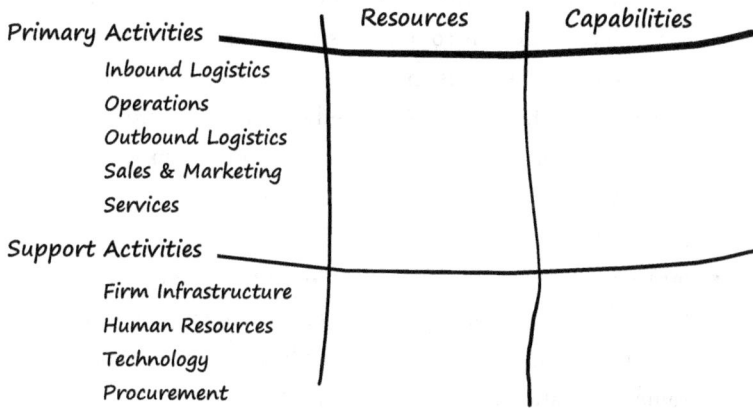

	Resources	Capabilities
Primary Activities		
Inbound Logistics		
Operations		
Outbound Logistics		
Sales & Marketing		
Services		
Support Activities		
Firm Infrastructure		
Human Resources		
Technology		
Procurement		

When to Use—Dissect Your Business Elements Around Primary and Secondary Activities

Porter's Value Chain Analysis guides businesses in discerning the processes that generate value by transforming inputs into outputs, ensuring that the value surpasses the original input costs. Understanding and optimizing the value creation process is fundamental to developing a competitive strategy that enhances competitive advantage and profitability. The first step is understanding where inputs generate the most value. A second step is being clear on where the company has a competitive advantage across the value chain, which allows for improved strategic focus.

Context and Scenario for Use

Porter's Value Chain Analysis is a strategic management tool used to examine a company's internal activities and understand how they create value and contribute to its competitive advantage. Here are some scenarios where Porter's Value Chain Analysis can be effectively utilized:

- **Industry Benchmarking and Competitive Analysis:** By dissecting the value chain into primary and support activities, organizations can compare their performance with that of competitors and identify areas where they excel or lag. For instance, a company may find its inbound logistics operations more efficient than its competitors, allowing it to negotiate better supplier contracts and reduce costs. Conversely, it may discover that its marketing and sales activities are less effective at reaching target customers, prompting investments in marketing strategies or distribution channels to improve competitiveness.

- **Strategic Planning and Decision Making:** When formulating their strategies, organizations must understand how each activity in the value chain contributes to their overall value proposition and competitive position. By systematically analyzing the value chain, organizations can identify opportunities to optimize processes, streamline operations, or differentiate products and services. For example, a company may identify opportunities to vertically integrate certain activities to gain greater control over quality or costs, or it may invest in research and development (R&D) to enhance product innovation and differentiation.

- **Supply Chain Management and Supplier Relationships:** Organizations can use this framework to assess the value added by different suppliers and identify opportunities for collaboration or cost savings. For instance, a company may collaborate closely with key suppliers to improve product quality, reduce lead times, or achieve economies of scale through joint purchasing agreements.

- **Cost Reduction:** Porter's Value Chain Analysis helps identify inefficiencies within various activities. Companies can improve their overall cost structure by focusing on areas where costs can be cut without sacrificing quality. This might include optimizing inbound logistics to reduce transportation costs or improving production processes to minimize waste.

- **Differentiation:** The value chain framework can highlight unique strengths in a company's operations that can be leveraged for differentiation. For example, superior customer service, innovative product development, or exceptional aftersales support can set a company apart. By understanding these strengths, companies can emphasize and enhance them to strengthen their market position.

- **Operational Improvement:** Continuous improvement is critical for maintaining competitiveness. Value Chain Analysis allows companies to pinpoint specific areas for operational enhancements. This could involve upgrading manufacturing technology, improving employee training programs, or enhancing communication across different departments to ensure smoother operations.

Porter's Value Chain Analysis is a versatile tool that you can apply in various strategic management contexts, including industry benchmarking, strategic planning, supply chain management, cost reduction, differentiation, and operational improvement. By dissecting the value chain and understanding how each activity contributes to competitive advantage, you can identify opportunities to enhance their overall competitiveness within their industry.

How to Use

A value chain represents a series of activities conducted by an organization to deliver value to its customers. It serves as a comprehensive tool for companies to assess and interconnect all their activities, offering insights into the sources of value within the organization.

Primary activities directly contribute to a product or service's physical creation, sale, maintenance, and support. These include:

1. **Inbound logistics:** Involves processes related to receiving, storing, and distributing internal inputs, with supplier relationships playing a crucial role in value creation.
2. **Operations:** Encompasses transformation activities converting inputs into sellable outputs, focusing on creating value through operational systems.
3. **Outbound logistics:** Covers activities such as delivering products or services to customers and involving internal or external collection, storage, and distribution systems.

4. **Marketing and sales** Encompass processes for persuading clients to choose the company over competitors. Value creation is linked to the benefits offered and effective communication.
5. **Service:** Includes activities related to maintaining the value of purchased products or services for customers.

Support activities underpin the primary functions and include:

1. **Procurement (purchasing):** Involves obtaining the necessary resources for operations, requiring effective vendor selection and negotiation.
2. **Human resource management:** Focuses on recruiting, hiring, training, motivating, rewarding, and retaining workers, recognizing the significance of people as a source of value.
3. **Technological development:** Encompasses activities managing and processing information, safeguarding a company's knowledge base, creating value through cost-effective IT, staying abreast of technological advances, and maintaining technical excellence.
4. **Infrastructure:** Involves a company's support systems and functions essential for daily operations, including accounting, legal, administrative, and general management, serving as valuable components businesses can leverage to their advantage.

Companies strategically utilize these primary and support activities as integral "building blocks" to create a valuable product or service. Dissecting the value chain helps them understand where value is created across the organization.

Notes for Your Use

- **Gather Data:** Collect valuable insights into your company's primary and secondary activities, establish connections with the RBV, and analyze resources and capabilities.
- **Evaluate Value:** Assess the value generated at the primary and secondary activity level, linking it to strengths identified in SWOT or SOAR.

- **Quantify Connections:** Quantify linkages and dependencies across your company to deepen your understanding of the interplay of activities.
- **Identify Opportunities:** Pinpoint potential areas for integrated value creation across various activities. Does integration necessitate retaining less valued activities?
- **Strategize:** Devise a strategic activity system by interconnecting activities and identifying the most valuable. Use VRIO to determine if the most valuable truly link to a competitive advantage.
- **Implement Strategy:** Implement a strategy to coordinate and maximize the value of activities effectively.

VRIO Analysis

Brief History

Jay Barney crafted the VRIO Analysis in "Firm Resources and Sustained Competitive Advantage."[6] Initially, Barney used the terms "Value," "Rareness," "Inimitability," and "Substitutability." The VRIO provides a methodology for assessing competitive advantage using these four basic analysis questions.

Model 5 of 50: The VRIO Flow Chart

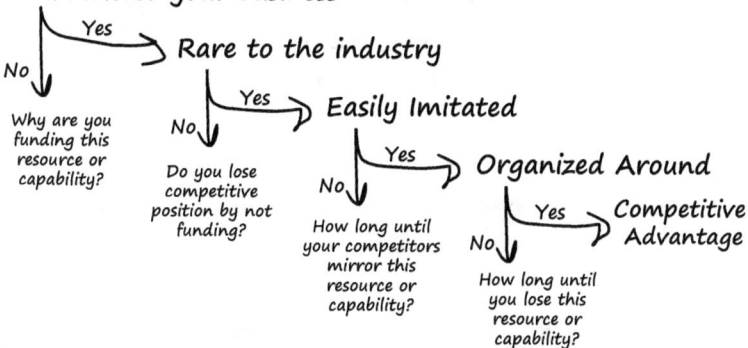

When to Use—Determine Your Competitive Advantage

VRIO builds upon the RBV and Porter's Value Chain Analysis to scrutinize an organization's resources, capabilities, and core competencies and determine whether they confer a competitive advantage. Not all resources, capabilities, and core competencies equate to sustained competitive advantage. VRIO discerns those that do and aids in identifying which of these elements should be reinforced in the business strategy. VRIO can also be tied to Porter's Value Chain to assess activities identified in the value chain analysis.

Context and Scenario for Use

VRIO is a strategic framework assessing resources, capabilities, and core competencies to determine competitive advantage and guide strategic decision making. Some examples of applications include:

- **Strategic Planning and Formulation:** When developing strategies, organizations must evaluate their resources and capabilities to identify those that are valuable, rare, inimitable, and organized to exploit opportunities and neutralize threats. By conducting a systematic VRIO analysis, organizations can prioritize investments and allocate resources to areas with a competitive advantage. For example, a company may find that its proprietary technology or patent portfolio gives it a distinct advantage over competitors, prompting further investment in R&D to maintain technological leadership.
- **Merger and Acquisition (M&A) Activities:** When considering acquiring or merging with another company, organizations must assess the target company's resources and capabilities to determine their potential for creating value. The VRIO analysis provides a framework for evaluating the strategic fit and compatibility of resources between the acquiring and target companies. This assessment helps identify potential synergies and risks associated with the M&A transaction, guiding decision-making and integration strategies.

- **Organizational Change and Renewal:** As industries evolve and market dynamics shift, organizations must continuously adapt to remain competitive. By leveraging their unique resources and capabilities identified through VRIO analysis, organizations can innovate and develop new products, services, or processes that create value for customers and differentiate them from competitors. For instance, a company may capitalize on its strong brand reputation or customer loyalty to successfully introduce new product lines or enter new markets.

- **Competitive Positioning:** In highly competitive markets, VRIO analysis helps organizations identify and focus on their unique strengths. By understanding which resources and capabilities are valuable, rare, inimitable, and organized, companies can develop strategies that enhance their market position and protect against competitive threats.

- **Resource Allocation:** VRIO analysis assists organizations in making informed decisions about where to allocate resources for maximum impact. By identifying which resources contribute most to competitive advantage, companies can prioritize investments that strengthen these areas and improve overall performance.

- **Strategic Alliances and Partnerships:** When forming strategic alliances or partnerships, organizations can use VRIO to assess the resources and capabilities of potential partners. This helps ensure the partnership creates mutual value and enhances both parties' competitive positions.

VRIO analysis is a powerful tool for various strategic management contexts, including strategic planning, M&A activities, organizational renewal, competitive positioning, resource allocation, and strategic alliance formation. By systematically evaluating internal resources and capabilities, you can identify your organization's competitive advantages and position your organization for long-term market success.

How to Use

Start with the RBV outputs of resources, capabilities, and core competencies or activities from Porter's Value Chain. Then, link to the VRIO elements. Follow this path, and ask the following questions about the resource, capability, or core competency:

1. **Is It Valuable?**
   - Consider if it enables implementing strategies to improve efficiency or effectiveness by exploiting opportunities or mitigating threats.
   - Assess Net Present Value (NPV) to ensure that costs invested are lower than expected future cash flows discounted back in time.
2. **If Yes, Is It Rare?**
   - Examine if it can only be acquired by one or a few companies, indicating rarity.
   - Competitive parity or equality arises if the resource is possessed by numerous industry players, leading to commonality.
3. **If Yes, Is It Costly to Imitate?**
   - Explore imperfections in imitation due to unique historical conditions, causal ambiguity, and social complexity.
   - *Unique Historical Conditions:* Decisions made in the past, known as path-dependency, impact a company's present and future options.
   - *Causal Ambiguity:* Arises when the connection between a company's controlled resources and its sustainable competitive advantage remains unclear.
   - *Social Complexity:* Refers to a company's reliance on social networks, culture, and reputation among suppliers and customers.
4. **Assess Organizational Support:**
   - Examine the organization's activities to ensure they support the resource, capability, or core competency.
   - Acknowledge that resources or capabilities alone yield advantages only if the organization has the structure to exploit and capture their value.

5. **If Yes, Sustained Competitive Advantage:**
   o Confirm that the organization, through supporting activities, maintains a sustained competitive advantage.

VRIO analysis provides a systematic method for discerning which resources, capabilities, and core competencies truly create competitive advantage and which do not.

Notes for Your Use

- **Start with Data:** Commence with information from your RBV and the SW components of SWOT or S from SOAR, incorporating insights from Competitor Analysis (Section 4).
- **Reinforce Insights:** Strengthen your viewpoint with Porter's Value Chain elements.
- **Apply Framework:** Apply the VRIO framework to evaluate your company's resources, capabilities, and core competencies. Discuss how the VRIO applies to each.
- **Focus on Key Areas:** Concentrate on resources, capabilities, and core competencies that offer a competitive advantage.
- **Implement Actions:** Implement actions focused on resources, capabilities, and core competencies to gain a competitive edge.

Kay's Distinctive Capabilities Framework

Brief History

Developed by John Kay, the Distinctive Capabilities Framework made its debut in his 1993 book, *Foundations of Corporate Success*.[7,8] Evolving from the RBV, this model presents an alternative perspective on competitive advantage to the VRIO analysis.

Model 6 of 50: The Distinctive Capabilities Table

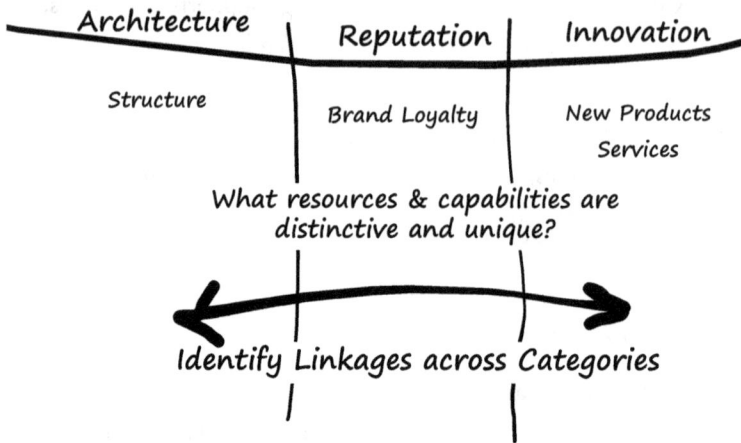

Architecture	Reputation	Innovation
Structure	Brand Loyalty	New Products Services

What resources & capabilities are distinctive and unique?

←——————————→

Identify Linkages across Categories

When to Use—Determine Your Competitive Advantage

The Distinctive Capabilities Framework delves into controlling three key capabilities—reputation, architecture, and innovation. Per Kay, reputation, architecture, and innovation pose challenges for competitors attempting imitation or replication. If skillfully leveraged, these factors can offer a sustained competitive advantage, a departure from other strategy frameworks that often emphasize control over strategic assets or resources.

Context and Scenario for Use

Evaluation of Kay's three key capabilities across competitive landscapes can be used in some of the following ways:

- **Strategic Analysis and Planning:** During strategic analysis and planning, organizations use Kay's framework to identify capabilities that differentiate them from competitors and contribute to success. This involves analyzing resources, skills, and competencies to pinpoint distinctive capabilities that provide a market edge, such as strong customer relationships, an innovative culture, or unique manufacturing processes.
- **Mergers, Acquisitions, and Strategic Partnerships:** When evaluating mergers, acquisitions, or strategic partnerships,

organizations assess the compatibility of their distinctive capabilities to determine potential value creation. Kay's framework helps evaluate the strategic fit and synergy between organizations, guiding decisions and partnership strategies. For instance, partnering with a firm with complementary capabilities can enhance mutual strategic objectives.

- **Organizational Renewal and Adaptation:** As industries and market dynamics evolve, organizations use Kay's framework to identify opportunities for growth and differentiation. By leveraging distinctive capabilities, such as new technological advancements or market expansions, organizations can adapt to changing conditions and maintain competitive advantage.

- **Competitive Positioning:** In competitive markets, Kay's framework helps organizations identify and emphasize capabilities that are hard for competitors to replicate, ensuring they maintain a strong market position.

- **Resource Allocation:** Kay's framework assists in prioritizing investments in capabilities that provide the most significant competitive advantage, guiding resource allocation to areas with the most significant impact.

Kay's Distinctive Capabilities Framework is valuable for strategic analysis, partnerships, and organizational renewal. By systematically identifying and leveraging distinctive capabilities, organizations can achieve long-term success and sustainable competitive advantage.

How to Use

According to Kay, a company's distinctive capability hinges on three key components:

1. **Architecture:** Encompasses the organizational structure, clear corporate objectives, and a focused workforce aligned with these objectives. It also includes the design of distribution channels and networks, contributing to the overall architecture.

2. **Reputation:** Reflects how customers and potential customers perceive the company. This is particularly crucial for companies offering quality products, as it is often shaped by customer experiences, advertising messages, and warranties.

3. **Innovation:** Recognizes innovation as a rare source of competitive advantage. It challenges companies to innovate consistently to enhance products or reduce costs.

These capabilities are challenging to cultivate and sustain, making them difficult for competitors to replicate. For effectiveness, they must be enduring and allowing the company to retain the added value it generates. Understanding a company's position on these capabilities provides insight into where competitive advantage exists.

Identify these three key components in your organization. Complete the table using resources and capabilities from RBV or activities from Porter's Value Chain Analysis.

Assess how the columns link and support one another.

Notes for Your Use

- **Gather Information:** Collect data on your organization's reputation, architecture, and innovation capabilities, including customer perceptions, organizational structure, distribution channels, and past innovation initiatives. Consider using your RBV or Porter's Value Chain Analysis as linkages.

- **Evaluate:** Assess the strength and uniqueness of your organization's reputation, architecture, and innovation capabilities compared to competitors. Identify areas of competitive advantage by linking to your VRIO analysis.

- **Connect:** Understand how your organization's distinctive capabilities contribute to its competitive advantage and market positioning. Explore connections between reputation, architecture, and innovation to identify synergies and areas for strategic alignment.

- **Develop Strategy:** Develop strategies to leverage and enhance your organization's distinctive capabilities. Identify opportunities to strengthen reputation further, optimize architecture, and foster innovation to maintain a competitive edge.

- **Implement Strategy:** Invest in reputation-building activities, restructure around organizational architecture advantage, and foster a culture of innovation.

SWOT Analysis

Brief History

The origins of the SWOT analysis can be traced back to Robert Franklin Stewart's SOFT (Satisfactory, Opportunity, Fault, and Threat) approach.[9-11] Replacing "satisfactory" and "fault" with strengths and weaknesses results in the SWOT of today. Both methods link an analysis of the organization's internal activities to the external environment.

Model 7 of 50: The SWOT Table

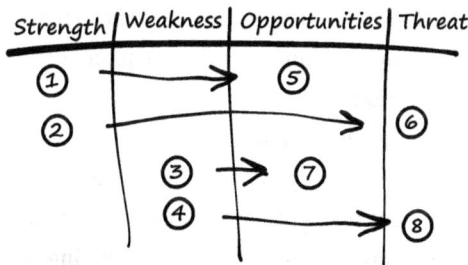

When to Use—Broadly Assess Your Business from Internal and External Perspectives

SWOT analysis evaluates an array of factors impacting a business's performance. These factors, categorized as internal (Strengths/Weaknesses) or external (Opportunities/Threats), can be favorable or unfavorable. SWOT provides a comprehensive tool for strategic assessment. It provides a broad view of the organization and its environment. The SWOT is most powerful when the internal and external components are linked.

Context and Scenario for Use

SWOT is a versatile tool used across business contexts. Some examples include:

- **Strategic Planning and Formulation:** During strategic planning and formulation, organizations use SWOT analysis to assess their internal capabilities and external environment. Organizations can capitalize on internal resources and competencies by identifying strengths, weaknesses, opportunities, and threats to gain a competitive advantage. This comprehensive assessment helps set strategic direction and adapt strategies to market trends, competitive pressures, and regulatory changes.

- **Market Entry and Expansion:** When considering entering new markets or launching new products, organizations use SWOT analysis to evaluate the viability and potential risks. By analyzing the attractiveness of the target market and identifying competitive advantages, organizations can anticipate challenges and barriers to entry. This analysis supports informed decision making regarding market entry strategies, resource allocation, and risk management.

- **Performance Evaluation and Improvement:** In performance evaluation, SWOT analysis helps organizations identify areas for improvement by regularly assessing their strengths, weaknesses, opportunities, and threats. This ongoing review enables organizations to enhance competitiveness and resilience by adapting strategies in response to market changes, ensuring long-term success and sustainability.

- **Strategic Decision Making:** SWOT analysis aids strategic decision making by providing insights into internal and external factors affecting the organization. It helps prioritize strategic initiatives, address weaknesses, leverage strengths, and capitalize on opportunities while mitigating threats.

- **Resource Allocation:** SWOT analysis informs resource allocation decisions by highlighting areas of strength and weakness. Organizations can prioritize investments in areas with the most significant potential for growth and improvement, ensuring the effective use of resources to support strategic objectives.

SWOT analysis is a versatile tool for strategic planning, market entry, performance evaluation, strategic decision making, and resource allocation. By systematically analyzing internal and external factors, you can gain valuable insights and develop effective strategies for achieving your organization's goals.

How to Use

By merging the internal and external dimensions, the SWOT analysis creates a table with four distinct columns: Strengths, Weaknesses, Opportunities, and Threats. The internal and external dimensions can be linked across these columns.

- **Strengths:** These factors set a company apart from competitors by representing its advantageous characteristics. They are often denoted as unique selling points (Section 3), firm-specific or competitive advantages (including resources, capabilities, and core competencies).
- **Weaknesses:** These encompass characteristics that place a company at a disadvantage relative to competitors (Section 4) and prove detrimental to its success. Examples include a lack of patent protection, a poor customer reputation, limited working capital, ineffective leadership, or an inefficient production process.
- **Opportunities:** External factors with the potential to positively impact a company's performance. Opportunities arise from elements in the external climate (Section 5) that can be exploited to gain an advantage.
- **Threats:** Conversely, threats are external factors (Section 5) that pose potential future challenges or obstacles for the company. Identifying and mitigating these threats is crucial for strategic planning and risk management.

Begin with an internal assessment of resources, capabilities, and core competencies to determine strengths and weaknesses—overlay competitive advantages against the competitive assessment. Then, assess the external environment within which the company operates. There is more on competitive advantage and climate in later sections (or Cs) of the toolbox.

SWOT reveals internal strengths, weaknesses, and external opportunities and threats—guiding strategic decisions, leveraging strengths, mitigating weaknesses, seizing opportunities, and managing threats for effective planning and execution.

Notes for Your Use

- **Gather Information:** Gather information to define the SWOT elements for your company.
- **Connect Elements:** Integrate your SW with RBV, VRIO, Kay's Framework, or Porter's Value Chain Analysis.
- **Evaluate Against Competitors:** Compare your SW against competitors.
- **Relate to Business Climate:** Relate Opportunities/Threats to the business climate.
- **Develop Strategy:** Develop a strategy linking strengths and weaknesses with opportunities and threats.
- **Implement Strategy:** Implement your strategy, leveraging strengths, mitigating weaknesses, seizing opportunities, and mitigating threats.

TOWS Analysis

Brief History

Heinz Weihrich introduced the TOWS Matrix in 1982 as an extension of SWOT analysis.[12] The TOWS Matrix emphasizes the relationship between external threats and opportunities before addressing internal strengths and weaknesses. It is a strategic tool for organizations to develop actionable strategies by aligning internal capabilities with external factors, enhancing their situational analysis. TOWS links directly to the SWOT table.

Model 8 of 50: The SWOT to TOWS Linkage

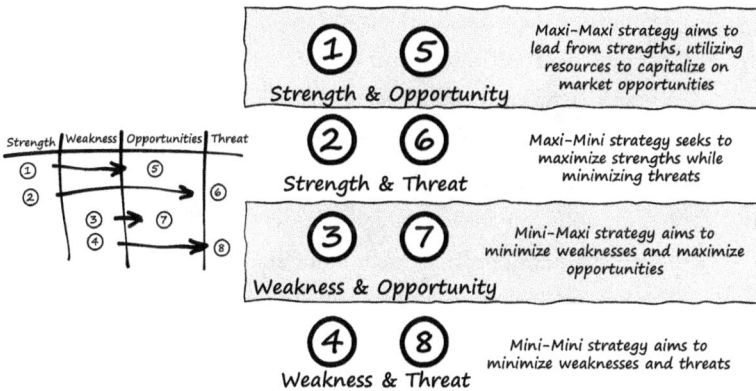

When to Use—Converting Your SWOT Analysis to Strategy

While a SWOT analysis evaluates a company's current internal and external landscape and allows the organization to assess future options, it doesn't prescribe specific strategic actions. The TOWS analysis is a complementary tool to map out potential strategic options, offering a structured approach to strategic planning and decision making from the SWOT basis. The SWOT converts information to insights and implications. The TOWS creates implementation strategies.

Context and Scenario for Use

TOWS aids in organizing the SWOT into strategic options. Similar to the SWOT, the TOWS has diverse applications. Some examples are provided below:

- **Strategic Planning and Formulation:** After conducting a SWOT analysis to identify internal strengths, weaknesses, opportunities, and threats, TOWS analysis helps formulate strategic options. The TOWS Matrix assists in leveraging strengths to capitalize on opportunities, addressing weaknesses to mitigate threats, and exploiting opportunities to overcome weaknesses. For instance, if a company has a strong brand reputation (strength) and there is increasing demand for eco-friendly products (opportunity), it might develop a strategy to launch a new line of sustainable products to capitalize on this trend.

- **Competitive Positioning and Differentiation:** In highly competitive or saturated markets, TOWS analysis helps organizations develop strategies to differentiate themselves and gain a competitive edge. By leveraging insights from TOWS, organizations can create strategies that exploit their strengths to seize market opportunities or counteract external threats. For example, if a company lacks skilled labor (weakness) but sees an increasing demand for customized solutions (opportunity), it could invest in employee training and develop personalized services to meet customer needs effectively.
- **Risk Management and Contingency Planning:** TOWS analysis is valuable for risk management and contingency planning. Organizations can develop strategies to mitigate risks and build resilience by proactively identifying potential threats and weaknesses. This approach allows organizations to anticipate challenges and uncertainties, adapt their strategies, and enhance their ability to navigate adverse conditions.
- **Strategic Decision Making:** TOWS analysis aids strategic decision making by matching internal capabilities with external conditions. It provides a structured approach to developing actionable strategies that address key issues, enhance competitive positioning, and align resources with strategic goals.
- **Resource Allocation:** The insights from a TOWS analysis guide resource allocation by identifying where strengths can be leveraged and weaknesses need to be addressed. This ensures that resources are invested in areas that will significantly impact achieving strategic objectives.

TOWS analysis is a powerful tool for strategic management. It applies to strategic planning, competitive positioning, risk management, and resource allocation. You can develop actionable strategies to your organizational goals and ensure long-term success by systematically aligning internal factors with external conditions.

How to Use

By integrating opportunities and threats from the external environment with the strengths and weaknesses of the internal organization, the TOWS Matrix formulates four fundamental strategic actions:

- **WT Strategy:** When a company faces limited development opportunities in a hostile environment with minimal potential for change and lacks significant strengths to withstand threats, the Mini-Mini strategy aims to minimize weaknesses and threats. This could involve scenarios ranging from pessimistic, such as liquidation, to optimistic, striving for survival through mergers.
- **WO Strategy:** When a company has more weaknesses but ample external opportunities, the Mini-Maxi strategy aims to minimize weaknesses and maximize opportunities. This involves exploiting external opportunities while addressing internal weaknesses, potentially through outsourcing or acquiring complementary companies.
- **ST Strategy:** When a robust company operates in a challenging environment, the Maxi-Mini strategy seeks to maximize strengths while minimizing threats. This may involve leveraging financial capabilities and cost-reducing skills to lower prices and drive out competition.
- **SO Strategy:** In an ideal scenario, a company maximizes its strengths and opportunities. The Maxi-Maxi strategy aims to lead from strengths, utilizing resources to capitalize on market opportunities. Companies in this position may consider international expansion or diversifying their product portfolio to enhance revenues.

TOWS analysis combines external threats and opportunities with internal strengths and weaknesses, guiding strategic actions that capitalize on strengths, address weaknesses, leverage opportunities, and manage threats.

Notes for Your Use

- **Merge Information:** Merge your SWOT into the TOWS.
- **Evaluate Alignment:** Examine the alignment of your current strategy with the TOWS.
- **Assess Effectiveness:** Evaluate with your team the effectiveness of this strategy in achieving high market share, profits, or growth.
- **Implement Strategic Actions:** Implement strategic actions as needed.

SOAR Analysis

Brief History

SOAR (Strengths, Opportunities, Aspirations, and Results) was developed by Jacqueline Stavros;[13] it was first published with David Cooperrider and D. Lynn Kelley in their paper "SOAR: A new approach to strategic planning," published in 2003.[14] A SOAR framework invites those into a strategic dialogue focused on an organization's strengths, opportunities, aspirations, and results to foster positive strategic thinking, planning, and leading to enhanced future performance.[15]

Model 9 of 50: **The SOAR Matrix**

Strengths	Opportunities	Aspirations	Results
What are we great at?	What are the possibilities?	What are our dreams and wishes?	What are meaningful outcomes?

When to Use—Broadening Your Business Alignment

SOAR is a strategic planning tool that creates a shared organizational vision for the future, aligning it with current strengths. This forward-focused, strengths-based approach refines an organization's core mission, purpose, and vision and fosters an action-oriented strategy by establishing connections between existing business conditions and future goals. The SOAR framework closely resembles the SWOT framework but is more positively focused and action oriented. However, SOAR and SWOT serve different purposes. SOAR is dialogically focused, while SWOT is more analytical.

Context and Scenario for Use

SOAR matrix is broad in application across different business contexts. Some scenarios for use include:

- **Organizational Change and Transformation:** During organizational change or transformation, SOAR engages employees and stakeholders in envisioning a desirable future. Organizations can drive change effectively by identifying and amplifying existing strengths, seizing emerging opportunities, articulating shared aspirations, and defining measurable results. For example, suppose an organization aims to lead in sustainability. In that case, SOAR can highlight strengths in innovation and stakeholder engagement, explore opportunities for eco-friendly products, set a shared aspiration for environmental stewardship, and establish measurable goals for reducing carbon footprint and increasing renewable energy usage.
- **Performance Improvement and Organizational Excellence:** In performance improvement, SOAR fosters a culture of positivity and continuous improvement. By focusing on strengths, opportunities, aspirations, and results rather than weaknesses or threats, organizations can build on their existing capabilities, leverage growth opportunities, and motivate employees with inspiring aspirations. For instance, to enhance customer satisfaction, SOAR can identify strengths in customer service, uncover opportunities for improving the customer experience, set a shared aspiration for customer delight, and define measurable metrics to track satisfaction improvements.
- **Cultural Transformation:** SOAR is valuable for cultural transformation by promoting a positive, forward-thinking

mindset. It helps organizations align their culture with strategic goals by emphasizing strengths and opportunities, articulating inspiring aspirations, and setting clear, results-oriented objectives. This approach supports a proactive and engaged workforce, driving cultural change and organizational growth.

- **Strategic Planning:** In strategic planning, SOAR assists in developing a vision and strategy by focusing on what the organization does well, what opportunities exist, what aspirations can drive success, and what results must be achieved. This positive approach supports creating a clear, actionable strategy that aligns with organizational goals.
- **Employee Engagement:** SOAR enhances employee engagement by involving teams in the process of defining strengths, opportunities, aspirations, and results. This inclusivity fosters a sense of ownership and commitment to achieving organizational goals, driving collective efforts toward success.

SOAR is a versatile framework for various strategic management contexts, including organizational change, performance improvement, cultural transformation, strategic planning, and employee engagement. You can drive positive change, foster growth, and effectively achieve strategic objectives by focusing on strengths, opportunities, aspirations, and results.

How to Use

Using the SOAR analysis involves a systematic approach within the four columns of the table, considering the current reality and future ambitions (adapted from Learnings to SOAR):

1. **Strengths:** Focus on your organization's existing strengths and unique attributes. Engage your team by asking questions like:
   - What are our current strengths?
   - What does our organization excel at?
   - What is our Unique Selling Proposition? Encourage customer involvement to uncover factors you may not be aware of.

   This column helps you double down on strengths.

2. **Opportunities:** Identify external opportunities in the marketplace that align with your strengths. Ask your team:
   ○ What trends can we capitalize on?
   ○ Are there partnerships or collaborations we can pursue?
   ○ Is there a market gap we could fill?
   This column helps you develop strategies to leverage external advantages for a broader market share.

3. **Aspirations:** Describe your organization's future and challenge the status quo. Ask your team:
   ○ What inspires our organization?
   ○ What do we hope to achieve?
   ○ What is our desired vision of the future?
   This column encourages innovative thinking and goal-setting, moving beyond routine and embracing new ideas.

4. **Results:** Define measurable results and target goals to track progress. Ask your team:
   ○ How does the organization track performance?
   ○ How do we convert aspirations into strategic initiatives (or SMART objectives)?
   ○ What tools do we need for success?
   The final column ensures a data-driven approach, using Key Performance Indicators (KPIs) or other performance management systems to confirm progress in your business model.

Incorporate insights from each column into a holistic strategic plan, aligning strengths with opportunities, challenging the status quo with aspirations, and setting measurable goals for results. Understanding the SOAR aids in clear communication across the organization.

Notes for Your Use

- **Gather Information:** Gather information to organize the four quadrants of the SOAR analysis; if you wish, you can start with your SWOT and TOWS.
- **Evaluate Situation:** Evaluate your present situation and envisioned future achievements.

- **Develop Plan:** Develop strategies or a strategic plan outlining your organization's specific focus areas.
- **Ensure Alignment:** Evaluate alignment between your strategy and the insights derived from the SOAR.
- **Implement Strategic Action:** Implement action to align your organization with the SOAR.

Company Checklist

The final model in Section 1 is a simple checklist that you and your team should consider when concluding the company evaluation step of your situation analysis. The table in Model 10 will help structure the discussion and link to the content within the first "C" of the toolbox.

Why a checklist?

Checklists foster team discussion by providing a structured framework for reviewing key analysis tasks. They prompt team members to share insights, identify potential challenges, and collaboratively problem-solve. Ensuring that all relevant items are covered, checklists encourage a thorough examination of the topic at hand, sparking conversation and promoting a shared understanding of objectives. Additionally, checklists empower team members to contribute their perspectives and expertise, enhancing communication and fostering a sense of ownership and collaboration within the team.

Model 10 of 50: Company Assessment Team Checklist

Question	Tools	Your team's thoughts
What is our Competitive Advantage?	RBV, Value Chain, VRIO, S (SWOT or SOAR)	
Are we organizing to sustain the Comp. Adv.?	RBV, Value Chain	
What opportunities exist to leverage our Comp. Adv.?	O (SWOT or SOAR)	
What threats exist to our Comp. Adv.? (vulnerabilities)	T (SWOT)	
Are we preparing to mitigate vulnerabilities?	TOWS	

SECTION 2

Characteristics: Still Factual and Controllable

Assess your offer strategy against the market of today and tomorrow.

Upon entering the "Characteristics" band, your level of control remains significant, albeit relying more on data derived from market research rather than purely factual knowledge. In this stage, your focus shifts to exploring how your products, services, or solutions generate value and understanding how this value evolves throughout their life cycle. The Characteristics band serves as a domain where you cultivate a profound comprehension of what you offer and its intricate connections to the marketplace.

Each model within this "C" provides a method for distilling information about the characteristics of your company's products and services. This segment delves into diverse perspectives on products and services, elucidating their intricacies intertwined with societal adoption rates. Understanding this life cycle and adoption rates is pivotal in allocating resources and prioritizing various time horizons for product and service offerings. Equally crucial is grasping the break-even points and price positioning of new offerings.

Subsequently, this section introduces a comprehensive view of your business offer. As with all sections, this section culminates with a checklist tool to facilitate group discussions concerning the Characteristic band.

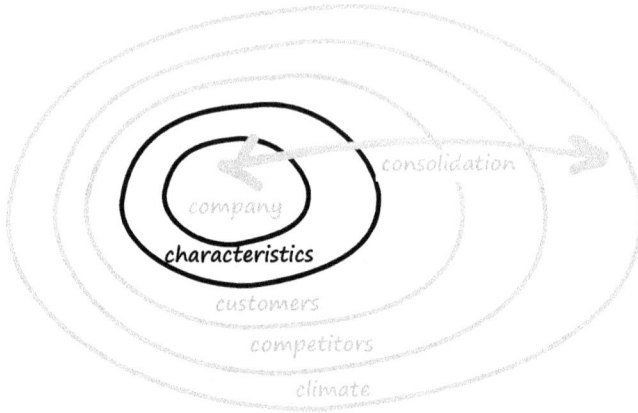

Quick exercise with your team:

Start your characteristics assessment the same way you did in the prior section. Conduct leadership interviews or a leadership workshop, and ask a few simple questions to understand your organization's starting point.

Questions:

- *Who buys from us today, and who do we want to buy from us tomorrow? Are these different?*
- *What are we offering these customers?*
- *Where are our products and services in their evolution? New or old to the customers?*
- *Who are the vital few—products and customers? What do we really care about?*
- *What are our break-even points? Do we measure them?*
- *What is the most resilient part of our portfolio? What is least?*

Kotler's 5 Product Levels

Brief History

Philip Kotler introduced the 5 Product Levels model in his marketing textbook *Marketing Management: Analysis, Planning, Implementation, and Control.*[16] This model was first outlined in the early editions of the book and has since become a fundamental concept in marketing theory and practice. Before publication in *Marketing Management*, Kotler and Sidney Levy introduced the concept of "Broadening the Concept of Marketing."[17] Through this model, Kotler aimed to provide marketers with a comprehensive framework for understanding the levels of product value and differentiation, guiding strategic decision making in product development, branding, pricing, and market positioning.

Model 11 of 50: 5 Product Levels

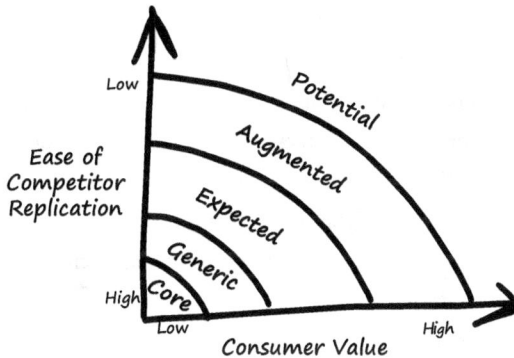

When to Use—Identify How to Expand Consumer Value

The 5 Product Levels model is a valuable tool for analyzing and comprehending the various levels of a product or service that customers perceive and value. This model enables businesses to tailor their marketing strategies effectively to meet customer needs. By aligning marketing strategies with each product level, companies can emphasize core benefits, promote generic product features, meet or exceed customer expectations, differentiate through augmented features, and plan for future innovations, ensuring a holistic approach to customer satisfaction and competitive positioning.

Context and Scenarios for Use

Kotler's 5 Product Levels model provides a versatile framework applicable across various industries and business contexts. Here are some scenarios where this model can be effectively utilized:

- **Market Entry Strategy:** Businesses can use the model to assess where their product fits within the competitive landscape (Section 4) when entering a new market. By understanding the level at which competitors operate, companies can position their offerings strategically to differentiate and capture market share while moving toward the outer levels.
- **Product Development:** During the product development process, the model helps identify opportunities for innovation and differentiation. By considering each level, product developers can brainstorm features and enhancements that elevate their offerings and create a competitive edge as the product offer moves toward the outer levels.
- **Brand Management:** Brands can leverage the model to evaluate how their products are perceived in the market. Understanding their products' current levels allows brands to develop branding and marketing strategies that communicate value and resonate with consumers, attempting to move outward across the levels.
- **Pricing Strategy:** The model informs pricing decisions by highlighting the perceived value of products at different levels. Companies can set prices that reflect the level of differentiation and justify premium pricing for products positioned at outer levels.
- **Customer Segmentation:** Businesses can tailor their product offerings to different market segments by analyzing customer preferences and behaviors. The model helps identify which products appeal to these segments based on their needs and preferences, with a focus on the outer levels.
- **Product Life Cycle Management:** The model guides decision making regarding product evolution and updates throughout the product life cycle. It ensures that products remain relevant and competitive by continuously innovating and moving toward the outer levels.

In summary, Kotler's 5 Product Levels model is a valuable tool for strategic decision making in various business aspects, including market entry, product development, branding, pricing, customer segmentation, and product life cycle management. Its versatility and comprehensiveness make it indispensable for businesses aiming to create and maintain competitive advantage in dynamic markets.

How to Use—Expand Your Product Offering Toward the Greatest Value

Starting with Kotler's 5 Product Levels model, evaluating your product offering through each lens is essential to strategize steps for reaching higher tiers of product differentiation and value. Delve into each level and discuss how to leverage them effectively with your products:

1. **Core-Level Products:** At this foundational level, products address fundamental consumer needs like sustenance (food), survival (water), or shelter. To strategize for higher tiers, focus on enhancing the core functionality and ensuring that your product fulfills these basic needs efficiently and effectively. Consider innovations that elevate the core offering, such as healthier food options or sustainable water solutions.

2. **Generic Level Products:** Generic products offer benefits beyond basic functionality but often lack differentiation, leading to price-based competition and commoditization. To move beyond this level, emphasize branding and marketing efforts to highlight unique selling points and create perceived value. Invest in product design, packaging, and branding to differentiate your offering from that of competitors and justify a premium price.

3. **Expected-Level Products:** Products at this level have additional value-adding features that differentiate them in the marketplace. However, they risk normalization over time, potentially reverting to core-level status. To prevent this regression and ascend to higher tiers, continually innovate and upgrade your product to maintain its relevance and desirability. Monitor consumer trends and feedback to identify areas for improvement and differentiation.

4. **Augmented Level Products:** Augmented products exhibit true differentiation in their respective markets, with features that contribute to a competitive advantage and enhance product appeal. To reach this level, focus on innovation and differentiation across all aspects of the product, including features, design, functionality, and customer experience. Invest in R&D to introduce groundbreaking features and technologies that set your product apart.

5. **Potential Products:** At the highest tier, potential products represent future transformations of augmented offerings, aiming to surprise and delight consumers through innovation and sustain brand equity. Regular updates and continuous innovation are essential to prevent falling to lower levels in the model. Engage in forward-thinking R&D to anticipate future consumer needs and preferences, stay ahead of the curve, and maintain a leadership position in the market.

By evaluating your product offering through the lens of Kotler's 5 Product Levels model and strategizing steps to reach higher tiers, you can effectively differentiate your products, create value for consumers, and maintain a competitive edge in the marketplace.

Notes for Your Use

- **Gather Information:** Collect data on your product's features, market position, and customer feedback.
- **Evaluate:** Use Kotler's 5 Product Levels model to assess your product's alignment with core, generic, expected, augmented, and potential levels.
- **Connect:** Identify connections between your product and each level to strategize differentiation and value creation. Does the team agree with the product placements across the model?
- **Develop Strategy:** Determine where movements across the model should occur. Create strategies tailored to enhance differentiation and value across all product levels.
- **Implement Strategy:** Execute initiatives such as product development and marketing to improve differentiation and maintain competitiveness at the outer levels.

Diffusion of Innovation

Brief History

In his 1962 book *Diffusion of Innovation*, Everett M. Rogers explored the spread of new ideas or technologies through communication channels over time.[18,19] The theory delineates the gradual process by which an idea or product gathers momentum and disseminates within a particular population or social system. The outcome of this diffusion is the adoption of a new idea, behavior, or product by individuals within the social framework.

Model 12 of 50: Diffusion of Innovation

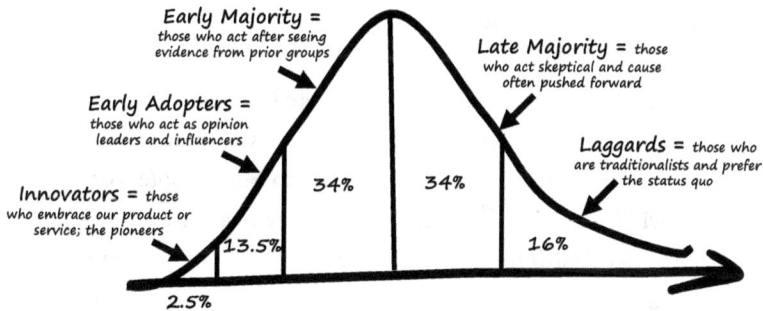

Early Majority = those who act after seeing evidence from prior groups

Late Majority = those who act skeptical and cause often pushed forward

Early Adopters = those who act as opinion leaders and influencers

Laggards = those who are traditionalists and prefer the status quo

Innovators = those who embrace our product or service; the pioneers

34%   34%

13.5%   16%

2.5%

When to Use—Determine Your Customer/Product Match

Rogers' Diffusion of Innovation theory is crucial for understanding the adoption of new technologies, be it smartphones, social media, or your newest product plans. This theory assists tech companies and marketers in pinpointing target audiences, crafting effective communication strategies, and steering the diffusion process. The foundational premise is that innovation adoption doesn't coincide in a social system; instead, it's a gradual process with varying adoption rates. Early adopters exhibit distinct characteristics from later ones. To successfully promote innovation, it's vital to grasp the target population's traits that either facilitate or impede the adoption process.

Context and Scenario to Use

Everett Rogers' Diffusion of Innovation theory provides valuable insights for marketers aiming to understand and influence the adoption of new products or innovations. Here are some scenarios where this theory can be effectively applied in marketing:

- **Product Launch Strategy:** When introducing a new product to the market, marketers can use the Diffusion of Innovation theory to identify and target innovators and early adopters—the first segments likely to embrace the innovation. By understanding their characteristics and preferences, marketers can tailor their messaging and channels to appeal to these influential groups, generating early momentum and word-of-mouth buzz.

- **Market Segmentation:** The theory helps segment the market based on the adoption curve, categorizing consumers into innovators, early adopters, early majority, late majority, and laggards. Marketers can develop targeted strategies for each segment, as customers in each segment have different needs. For example, they can offer incentives to early adopters or provide social proof to convince the early majority.

- **Product Positioning:** Understanding where a product falls on the adoption curve informs its positioning strategy. For instance, if a product targets innovators and early adopters, emphasizing novelty, cutting-edge features, and exclusivity can appeal to this segment. Conversely, positioning strategies for the early and late majority may focus on reliability, convenience, and social proof.

- **Communication Strategy:** Different market segments respond to different messaging and communication channels. Marketers can leverage the diffusion of innovation theory to craft communication strategies that resonate with each segment's values, preferences, and communication channels. For example, they can use social media influencers to reach early adopters or testimonials from mainstream users to appeal to the early majority.

- **Product Life Cycle Management:** The diffusion of innovation theory helps marketers understand how a product's adoption evolves. Marketers can anticipate changes in consumer behavior and preferences as the product moves through the adoption curve, adjusting their marketing strategies accordingly to maintain momentum and extend the product's life cycle.

Overall, Everett Rogers' Diffusion of Innovation theory provides marketers with a systematic framework for understanding the adoption process and developing targeted strategies to accelerate the acceptance and diffusion of new products in the market.

How to Use

To identify a product or technology's position on the diffusion curve, it's essential to examine its current market penetration and momentum. The adopter categories play a pivotal role in understanding this dynamic process. The five categories are:

1. **Innovators:** These pioneers are the first to embrace innovations. Driven by a sense of adventure and a high tolerance for uncertainty, they play a crucial role in testing and promoting new ideas.
2. **Early Adopters:** Opinion leaders and influencers within their social networks, early adopters adopt innovations relatively early and serve as role models for others.
3. **Early Majority:** Pragmatists who adopt innovations after seeing evidence of their benefits, the early majority are deliberate decision makers who rely on the experiences of early adopters.
4. **Late Majority:** Typically skeptical and cautious, the late majority adopts innovations after most others have done so, often influenced by social pressure or necessity.
5. **Laggards:** The most resistant to change are traditionalists, who prefer established practices and may adopt innovations only when they have no alternative.

The stages through which individuals adopt an innovation are essential to understand as the individual traverses the five stages:

1. **Knowledge:** Awareness of the innovation's existence without detailed information.

2. **Persuasion:** Seeking more information and evaluating potential benefits and drawbacks.
3. **Decision:** Choosing to adopt or reject the innovation based on perceived advantages and compatibility.
4. **Implementation:** Putting the innovation into practice and overcoming practical challenges.
5. **Confirmation:** Assessing the experience and confirming the decision to adopt based on outcomes.

The five main factors influencing adoption are:

1. **Relative Advantage:** The perceived superiority of the innovation over what it replaces.
2. **Compatibility:** Consistency with potential adopters' values, experiences, and needs.
3. **Complexity:** The difficulty of understanding or using the innovation.
4. **Trialability:** The extent to which the innovation can be tested before commitment.
5. **Observability:** The visibility of tangible results from the innovation.

Factors vary in influence across the adopter categories, shaping the diffusion process. Understanding the factors aids in addressing the needs of specific adoption categories.

Adoption can be influenced through the interplay of factors of influence, stages, and categories.

Notes for Your Use

- **Gather Information:** Collect data on the product's market penetration and momentum to understand its position on the diffusion curve.
- **Evaluate:** Assess the product's adoption across innovators, early adopters, early majority, late majority, and laggards, understanding their roles and behaviors in the diffusion process.

- **Connect:** Identify connections between the product's adoption stages and the adopter categories, recognizing how each group progresses through knowledge, persuasion, decision, implementation, and confirmation.
- **Develop Strategy:** Formulate strategies based on factors influencing adoption, including relative advantage, compatibility, complexity, trialability, and observability. Tailor approaches to each adopter category.
- **Implement Strategy:** Execute initiatives such as targeted marketing campaigns, educational efforts, and product demonstrations to accelerate adoption across different adopter categories.

Product Life Cycle Stages

Brief History

The International Product Life Cycle, developed by economist Raymond Vernon in 1966, remains a prominent model in economics and marketing.[20] This model outlines distinct stages that products undergo, from market entry to eventual decline. Raymond Vernon posits that each product follows a specific life cycle, commencing with development and concluding with decline.

Model 13 of 50: Product Life Cycle

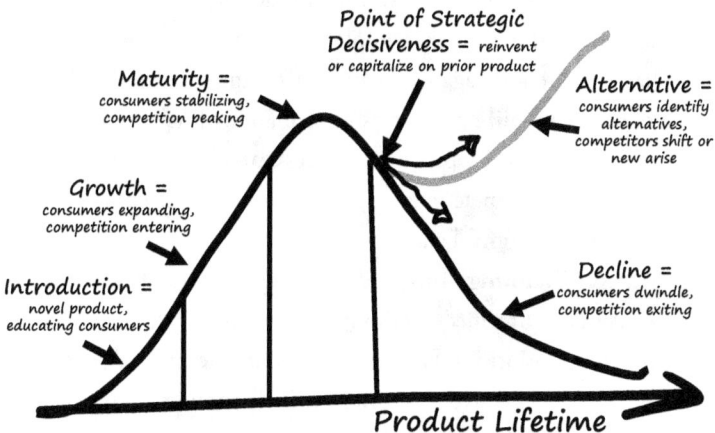

Point of Strategic
Decisiveness = reinvent
or capitalize on prior product

Maturity =
consumers stabilizing,
competition peaking

Alternative =
consumers identify
alternatives,
competitors shift or
new arise

Growth =
consumers expanding,
competition entering

Introduction =
novel product,
educating consumers

Decline =
consumers dwindle,
competition exiting

Product Lifetime

When to Use—Determine Your Product's Life Cycle Evolution

The Product Life Cycle serves as a marketing framework, providing insight into the sales trajectory of a product category over time. Analogous to the life cycle of living organisms, products experience a journey from inception to eventual discontinuation. This life cycle is visually represented through a graph, depicting sales from the product category's market entry to its exit. The Product Life Cycle divides product sales into four phases: Introduction, Growth, Maturity, and Decline. The key objective of the Product Life Cycle is determining when to make a point of strategic decisiveness, whereby the company moves from the current product to the new alternative.

Context and Scenario to Use

Raymond Vernon's product life cycle theory offers valuable insights for businesses developing strategic plans for their products. Here are some contexts and scenarios where this theory can be applied:

- **New Product Development:** Businesses can use the product life cycle concept to guide their new product development efforts. By understanding the stages of introduction, growth, maturity, and decline, companies can anticipate future market dynamics and design products positioned to succeed throughout their life cycle or reposition toward the end.
- **Market Entry Strategy:** When entering a new market, companies can assess the stage of the product life cycle to inform their entry strategy. For example, entering during the growth phase may require aggressive marketing and distribution efforts to capitalize on increasing demand, while entering during the maturity phase may necessitate differentiation strategies to compete in a saturated market where competitors likely already control scale.
- **Strategic Planning:** The product life cycle model helps businesses make informed decisions about resource allocation and investment priorities. For instance, companies may allocate more resources to R&D during the introduction phase to capitalize on innovation opportunities while focusing on cost

efficiency and streamlining operations during the maturity
and decline phases to maximize profitability.

- **Marketing and Promotion:** Different product life cycle
stages require different marketing and promotion strategies.
During the introduction phase, companies may create awareness and educate consumers about the new product's benefits. In the growth phase, marketing efforts may shift toward
building brand loyalty and expanding market share. During
maturity, companies may implement promotional tactics such
as price discounts or product bundling to maintain market
share and combat competition.

- **Product Portfolio Management:** Businesses with multiple
product lines can use the product life cycle model to assess the
health of their product portfolio and make decisions about
product divestment, extension, or innovation across the life
cycle of a portfolio of products. Companies can develop strategies to optimize their portfolio's overall performance and lon-
gevity by understanding where each product falls within its life
cycle and when to act upon the point of strategic decisiveness.

In summary, Raymond Vernon's product life cycle theory provides
businesses with a framework for understanding the dynamics of product
evolution, planning strategic initiatives to maximize success throughout
each stage of the product's life cycle, and ultimately making the strategic
decision to move forward with the alternative product.

How to Use

Product Life Cycle Management involves strategically overseeing the development, manufacturing, sales, and marketing of a product through
its distinct life stages, where sales, investments, profits, and competition
evolve. The life cycle consists of four phases:

- **Introduction:** In this initial phase, the product category is
novel, and market awareness is low. Sales grow slowly due
to limited marketing and consumer reluctance. Typically, a

single pioneer company enters with either a high-price strategy (Skimming) or a low-price strategy (Penetration Pricing). Competition is minimal, and profits are low. Risks are high.

- **Growth:** During the Growth phase, the market expands rapidly, and early growth exhibits steep sales escalation. Intense competition emerges as new players introduce similar products. The Late Growth phase sees sales plateau, marking the transition to Maturity. Scale advantage becomes clearer.
- **Maturity:** At Maturity, sales stabilize, and tapping new market segments becomes challenging. Competition peaks, resulting in a "Shakeout," with surviving companies striving to maintain market share. Consolidation begins. Profits are high due to reduced investment needs and economies of scale.
- **Decline:** As market needs change or superior alternatives arise, the Decline phase begins. Sales and profitability dwindle, and surviving in a shrinking market becomes challenging. Companies face decisions on whether to sustain investments or exit the declining market. Consolidation offers a method to succeed.

Each phase entails unique sales levels, investment requirements, competition intensity, and profit potential. Navigating these stages effectively and knowing when to take the strategic decision to pivot to an alternative is crucial as you seek sustained success in dynamic markets.

Notes for Your Use

- **Gather Information:** Collect data on each product's stage in the product life cycle model. Also, collect information on market dynamics, sales trends, competition, and consumer preferences.
- **Evaluate:** Assess each product's position within its life cycle stage and its implications. Discuss the level of market saturation, growth potential, and competitive intensity.
- **Connect:** Discuss how each stage influences decisions related to product development, market entry strategies, resource allocation, marketing, promotion, and product portfolio management.

- **Develop Strategy:** Develop strategies tailored to each product's life cycle stage and assess the signpost that indicates a point of strategic decisiveness when the movement to an alternative should occur.
- **Implement Strategy:** Implement strategic initiatives such as targeted marketing campaigns, product development efforts, market expansion plans, and portfolio optimization strategies.

Break-Even Analysis

Brief History

The concept of Break-Even Analysis has evolved, with various contributors making significant contributions. The first break-even chart to appear in the Accounting Review was presented by James Dohr in 1932.[21] Break-Even Analysis is a valuable tool for examining the correlation between fixed costs, variable costs, and revenue. It is intricately connected to the Break-Even Point, signifying the juncture at which an investment begins yielding a positive return.

Model 14 of 50: Break-Even Analysis

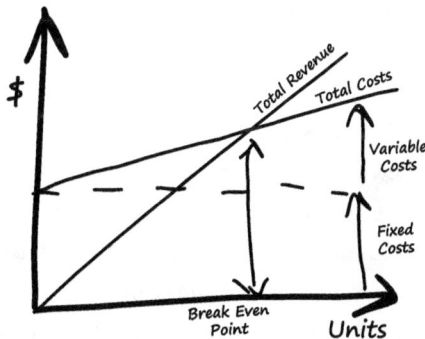

Formula

$$\text{Break Even Point (Units)} = \frac{\text{Fixed Cost}}{(\text{Price Per Unit} - \text{Variable Cost per Unit})}$$

$$\text{Break Even Point (Price per Unit)} = (\text{Fixed Cost} / \text{Units}) + (\text{Variable Cost} / \text{Units})$$

When to Use—Assess Your Break-Even Point and Understand the Key Sensitivities

Break-Even Analysis evaluates the risk and value of business investments, particularly in expanding operations, growing product offers, or entering new markets. It aids in understanding the time required for an investment to turn profitable and determining the minimum sales needed to cover costs. When adjusting pricing, Break-Even Analysis helps calculate additional units required to offset decreases. Break-Even Analysis simplifies complex scenarios in decision-making, offering business leaders clarity. It reveals the point at which an investment breaks even, ensuring a dollar-for-dollar return, streamlining decision-making, and mitigating risks associated with various business scenarios.

Context and Scenario to Use

Break-Even Analysis is a fundamental tool used in business to assess the feasibility of a product, service, or project by determining the point at which total revenues equal total costs, resulting in neither profit nor loss. This analysis provides you valuable insights into pricing strategies, cost management, and decision-making in various contexts. Here are some use scenarios:

- **New Product Launch:** When introducing a new product to the market, Break-Even Analysis helps assess the minimum level of sales required to cover initial investment costs. By calculating the Break-Even Point, businesses can determine the pricing strategy or sales level needed to achieve profitability and evaluate the product's viability in the market.
- **Investment Evaluation:** Break-Even Analysis helps evaluate potential investments or projects by comparing expected revenues against associated costs. It helps businesses assess the risk and return of different investment opportunities and prioritize those with the shortest break-even period or highest potential profitability.

- **Cost Management:** Break-Even Analysis aids in cost management by identifying cost structures and understanding their impact on profitability. By analyzing fixed and variable costs, businesses can identify opportunities to reduce costs and improve efficiency, ultimately lowering the Break-Even Point and increasing profitability.
- **Price Setting:** Break-Even Analysis informs pricing decisions by providing insights into the relationship between price, volume, and profitability. By understanding the cost structure and Break-Even Point, businesses can optimize price scenarios that cover costs, maximize profit margins, and remain competitive.
- **Scenario Planning:** Break-Even Analysis facilitates scenario planning by allowing businesses to assess the impact of different variables on profitability. By conducting sensitivity analysis, companies can evaluate the effect of changes in sales volume, costs, or pricing on the Break-Even Point and adjust their strategies accordingly to mitigate risks and capitalize on opportunities.

In summary, Break-Even Analysis is a versatile tool that provides valuable insights into pricing, cost management, investment evaluation, and decision-making in various business contexts. It enables you to assess project feasibility, optimize pricing strategies, and make informed decisions to achieve profitability and sustainable growth.

How to Use

Break-Even Analysis is a crucial financial assessment for determining a company's Break-Even Point. This calculation involves fixed and variable costs in relation to unit price and profit. Fixed costs, such as rent, equipment, salaries, interest, taxes, and insurance, remain constant regardless of sales volume. Variable costs fluctuate with sales, including labor, raw materials, commissions, utilities, and shipping. The Break-Even Point is the sum of labor and material costs to produce one unit.

The Break-Even Point reveals the number of units a company needs to sell to cover both fixed and variable costs, achieving a Break-Even Point where total revenue equals total costs.

For businesses, Break-Even Analysis is pivotal in decision-making, aiding in pricing strategies, cost management, and risk assessment. By understanding the quantity of units needed to cover costs, companies can set realistic sales targets, assess the impact of pricing changes, and evaluate the financial viability of various scenarios. This analysis is a valuable tool for start-ups, product launches, or when considering changes in pricing structures, offering a quantitative foundation for strategic decisions and financial planning.

Notes for Your Use

- **Gather Information:** Collect data on fixed and variable costs, unit selling prices, and sales volume projections.
- **Evaluate:** Discuss the financial feasibility of projects or products by calculating the Break-Even Point and analyzing its implications for profitability.
- **Connect:** Assess the Break-Even Analysis with broader product strategies and conduct sensitivity analysis to understand how variable changes impact the calculation.
- **Develop Strategy:** Based on Break-Even Analysis, develop pricing strategies, cost management plans, and investment priorities.
- **Implement Strategy:** Monitor the key variables within the sensitivity analysis as you launch in a way that ensures the resiliency of the break-even calculation.

Pareto Analysis

Brief History

The general concept of the Pareto Principle, or the 80/20 rule, is widely attributed to Vilfredo Pareto's study of landownership concentrated. The Pareto Principle was later generalized and expanded to apply widely in areas where 80 percent of problems or product sales can be attributed to 20 percent of causes or customers. Stated differently, 20 percent of the causes lead to 80 percent of the effects. This principle has become a cornerstone for understanding and addressing issues efficiently by focusing on the vital few.

Model 15 of 50: Pareto Analysis

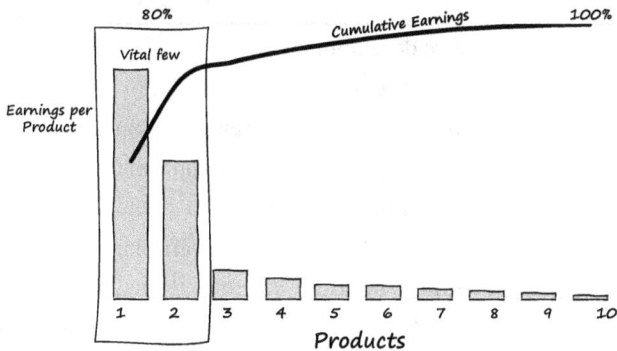

When to Use—Identify the Vital Few or What Is Important

Utilize the Pareto analysis when assessing customer concentration and revenue distribution. If 80 percent of revenues come from 20 percent of customers, the principle suggests focusing efforts on that vital few 20 percent. This analysis helps businesses evaluate whether sales are concentrated in a select few customers or spread across a diversified customer base.

Context and Scenario to Use

Pareto analysis is a valuable tool for product analysis, particularly in identifying and prioritizing key factors contributing to product performance, customer satisfaction, and profitability. Here's how Pareto analysis can be applied in product analysis:

- **Identifying Key Product Issues:** Pareto analysis helps businesses identify the most significant issues or factors impacting product performance or customer satisfaction. By analyzing data on product defects, customer complaints, or returns, businesses can identify the top 20 percent of issues that account for 80 percent of product-related problems. This insight allows businesses to focus their efforts and resources on addressing the vital few issues first, leading to more significant improvements in product quality and customer experience.

- **Prioritizing Product Enhancements:** When planning product enhancements or new features, Pareto analysis helps businesses prioritize development efforts based on the features that significantly impact customer satisfaction or market demand. By identifying the top 20 percent of features that drive 80 percent of product value or usage, businesses can focus on enhancing those features to meet customer needs effectively and differentiate their product from competitors.

- **Optimizing Product Portfolio:** Pareto analysis aids in optimizing product portfolios by identifying the most profitable products or product lines. Businesses can locate the top-performing products that generate the most revenue or profits by analyzing sales data, revenue contribution, and profitability margins. This insight allows companies to allocate resources more effectively, investing in product lines with the highest potential for growth and profitability while phasing out or repositioning underperforming products.

- **Customer Portfolio:** Similar to the product portfolio, in repeat customer markets, assessing customer purchases using the Pareto analysis identifies the few most important customers that generate the most significant business return, volume, or value. These vital few are the company's key customers.

In summary, Pareto analysis provides a systematic approach to product analysis by identifying and prioritizing key factors influencing product performance, customer satisfaction, and profitability. By focusing on the most critical issues or opportunities, you can make more informed decisions, allocate resources more effectively, and drive continuous improvement in product quality and competitiveness.

How to Use

To conduct a Pareto analysis for customer or product prioritization, follow these steps:

1. **Data Extraction:** Begin by extracting revenue data at the customer or product level.
2. **Ranking:** Rank the data from largest to smallest based on revenue contribution.
3. **Graphical Representation:** Create a bar graph illustrating individual revenue contributions and a cumulative line graph.
4. **Assess Cumulative Revenue:** Evaluate the cumulative line graph to identify where 80 percent of total revenue is reached.
5. **Identify the "Vital Few":** Focus on the "vital few"—the top customers or products contributing the first 80 percent of cumulative revenue.
6. **Consider Concentration:** If a small percentage of customers or products (e.g., 20 percent) contributes to a significant portion (80 percent) of the revenue, it suggests concentration.

Pareto analysis helps prioritize efforts on your business's most impactful aspects, ensuring a concentrated focus on the key revenue contributors. Although this analysis is focused on your company's products, it can be used broadly.

Notes for Your Use

- **Gather Information:** Collect data to analyze, for example, product defects, customer complaints, returns, sales data, revenue contribution, and profitability margins.
- **Evaluate:** Analyze the data following the model to identify the top 20 percent of factors contributing to 80 percent.
- **Connect:** Discuss the graphical output with your team to determine if the model accurately fits.
- **Develop Strategy:** Discuss strategic options addressing both the vital few and the many others, focusing on the

competitive advantage within the vital few or the ability to move toward diversification into the many (the other 80 percent).

- **Implement Strategy:** Continue aligning with McKinsey Three Horizons and BCG Growth-Share Matrix to ensure long-term portfolio health beyond the current vital few.

BCG Growth-Share Matrix

Brief History

The Boston Consulting Group (BCG) Growth-Share Matrix, introduced by Bruce Henderson in 1970 in *The Product Portfolio*, is a strategic tool for companies to allocate investments effectively across their product portfolios.[22] The BCG matrix aids companies in assessing the portfolio of products across different growth rates and market shares to balance in total and in a way such that the four different quadrants support one another for total portfolio long-term resilience.

Model 16 of 50: BCG Growth-Share Table

4 matrix quadrants	Relative Market Share	Market Growth Rate	Cash Generation	Resource Allocation
Stars	High market share, look for comp. adv.	High market growth rate, check lifecycle	Generate most cash	Consume a lot of cash
Cash Cows	High market share	Low market growth rate	Significant cash	Invest to maintain
Question Marks	Low market share	High market growth rate	Consume cash	Potential Star, allocate to grow share
Pets (commonly Dogs)	Low market share	Low market growth rate	Declining cash	Decrease resources faster than cash decline

When to Use—Focus on the Categorization of Your Products or Business Units

The BCG Growth-Share Matrix guides corporate strategy by analyzing business units based on relative market share and growth rate. Categorizing units as "Stars," "Cash Cows," "Question Marks," or "Dogs" aids in resource allocation decisions, as well as direct investments, divestments, and cash flow. This strategic tool informs companies on where to focus and optimizes their portfolio.

Context and Scenario to Use

BCG Growth-Share Matrix is a strategic tool designed to help businesses analyze their product portfolio and make decisions regarding resource allocation and strategic direction. It classifies products into four categories based on their market growth rate and relative market share, providing insights into each product's strategic importance and potential for future growth. Here's how the BCG Growth-Share Matrix can be applied in different contexts:

- **Portfolio Analysis:** The BCG Growth-Share Matrix is commonly used for portfolio analysis, where businesses evaluate their product portfolio's performance and strategic position. Evaluate products based on their market growth rate and market share, and companies can identify which products are stars (high growth, high market share), cash cows (low growth, high market share), question marks (high growth, low market share), or dogs (low growth, low market share). This analysis helps businesses understand the overall health of their portfolio and make informed decisions about resource allocation and investment priorities.
- **Strategic Planning:** The BCG Growth-Share Matrix informs strategic planning by highlighting areas of opportunity and risk within the product portfolio. For example, stars represent products with high growth potential that require investment to maintain their growth trajectory. Cash cows generate significant revenue but have low growth prospects, allowing businesses to allocate profits toward other business areas. Question marks require careful consideration, as they have high growth potential but low market share, requiring

strategic investments to capitalize on opportunities. Dogs may need to be divested or repositioned to minimize losses and focus resources on more promising products.

- **Marketing Strategy:** The BCG Growth-Share Matrix guides marketing strategy by providing insights into product positioning and market competitiveness. Businesses can tailor marketing efforts based on each product's strategic position within the matrix. For example, stars may benefit from aggressive marketing campaigns to capitalize on their high growth potential and strengthen their market position. Cash cows may require more defensive marketing strategies to maintain market share and maximize profitability. Question marks may benefit from market development or product differentiation strategies to increase market share and improve competitiveness.

- **Resource Allocation:** The BCG Growth-Share Matrix helps businesses allocate resources effectively by aligning investment decisions with the strategic priorities of each product category. By categorizing products based on their growth potential and market share, companies can allocate resources proportionally to each category. They can invest in stars to fuel growth, milk cash cows to generate profits, and carefully manage question marks and dogs to minimize risks and losses.

In summary, the BCG Growth-Share Matrix is a versatile tool that provides valuable insights into portfolio management, strategic planning, marketing strategy, and resource allocation. By categorizing products based on their market growth rate and relative market share, businesses can make informed decisions to drive growth, maximize profitability, and enhance competitiveness in the marketplace.

How to Use

Creating a BCG Growth-Share Matrix involves collecting data on your products' market share and growth, comparing them with major competitors, and analyzing future growth projections. The matrix's four categories are Question Marks, Stars, Cash Cows, and Dogs, each representing a specific relative market share and growth combination.

- **Low Growth, High Share (Cash Cows):** Milk these products for cash to reinvest elsewhere. They generate more cash than their cash allocation needs. Do not invest back in the Cash Cow solely.
- **High Growth, High Share (Stars):** Significantly invest in these products with high future potential.
- **High Growth, Low Share (Question Marks):** Decide whether to invest or discard these products based on their chances of becoming stars. Develop clear market assessment methods to determine question mark progression.
- **Low Share, Low Growth (Pets or Dogs):** Liquidate, divest, or reposition these products.

Relevant strategies for each category:

- **Build the Product:** Invest to increase market share, suitable for Question Marks aiming to become Cash Cows.
- **Hold the Product:** Leave a product for some time, applicable to Star Products when additional investment isn't possible.
- **Divest:** Release cash tied to unprofitable products, ideal for Dogs.
- **Harvest:** Reduce investments to maximize cash inflow, which is beneficial for Cash Cows and enhances overall profitability.

By strategically placing products within these categories, you can make informed decisions about where to allocate your organization's resources, invest, or divest, ensuring a balanced and profitable product portfolio.

Notes for Your Use

- **Gather Information:** For each product in the portfolio, collect data on market share, growth rates, and competitor performance.

- **Evaluate:** Analyze the data to determine each product's relative market share and growth, categorizing them into the model table. Conduct a quick Pareto analysis to determine where the 80/20 reside.
- **Connect:** Identify connections between products' positioning in the table categories and their resource allocation and cash generation. Discuss if the resources and cash generation logically align with the category.
- **Develop Strategy:** Develop strategies tailored to each category. Consider the product life cycle for each category.
- **Implement Strategy:** Continue assessing the balance of the overall portfolio and aligning with McKinsey Three Horizons to ensure long-term portfolio health.

McKinsey's Three Horizons of Growth

Brief History

Introduced in *The Alchemy of Growth: Practical Insights for Building the Enduring Enterprise*, McKinsey's Three Horizons of Growth offers a strategic roadmap to bridge the gap between current profitability (Horizon 1), future business aspirations (Horizon 3), and the steps required for transition (Horizon 2).[23] The Three Horizons Framework ensures a balanced focus on current and future needs, guiding businesses toward sustainable growth.

Model 17 of 50: McKinsey's Three Horizons of Growth Table

Horizon	Business Allocation	Lifecycle	Comp. Advantage
Horizon 1 = Core businesses of today Horizon 2 = Next-up opportunities Horizon 3 = Future options	Where are your resources and profits allocated across the horizons?	Where on the Product Lifecycle do your bets in each horizon reside?	What is your competitive advantage in each horizon? What are the opportunities and threats to each horizon?

When to Use—Balance Your Portfolio Toward the Current and Future

McKinsey's Three Horizons Framework is a strategic planning approach designed to assist organizations in navigating their growth strategy and unleashing transformative potential. This framework adopts an adaptive management approach, categorizing growth into three horizons. These horizons serve as a guide for recognizing and addressing shifts in the business environment. Organizations can allocate resources and attention across the three horizons by applying this framework to product strategy. McKinsey's Three Horizons Framework provides a roadmap for your product strategy, guiding your organization in balancing incremental improvements with breakthrough innovations. The Three Horizons Framework ensures a broad focus across products or customer sectors, not an overly focused emphasis on the current core.

Context and Scenario to Use

McKinsey's Three Horizons Framework offers a versatile tool for strategic planning across various contexts and scenarios. Here are some key applications:

- **Corporate Strategy:** Organizations can use the Three Horizon Framework to align their corporate strategy with long-term growth objectives. Horizon 1 focuses on optimizing existing business operations and maximizing short-term performance. Horizon 2 explores emerging opportunities and innovations that have the potential to become future growth engines. Horizon 3 encourages experimentation and investment in disruptive innovations that could shape the company's future direction.
- **Innovation Management:** The framework helps businesses manage their innovation portfolios effectively. Horizon 1 innovations involve incremental improvements to existing products or processes to maintain competitiveness and efficiency. Horizon 2 innovations explore new markets or technologies that offer growth opportunities beyond the current business

scope. Horizon 3 innovations involve radical, transformative ideas that may disrupt existing markets or create new ones.

- **Product Development:** When planning product development strategies, organizations can use the Three Horizons Framework to balance short-term revenue generation with long-term innovation. Horizon 1 products focus on meeting current customer needs and improving existing offerings. Horizon 2 products explore adjacent markets or new features that address emerging trends or customer preferences. Horizon 3 products involve breakthrough innovations that may fundamentally change how customers interact with the company's products or services.

- **Resource Allocation:** The framework aids resource allocation by providing a structured approach to prioritizing investments across different time horizons. Organizations can allocate resources based on the potential impact and risk associated with initiatives on each horizon. For example, Horizon 1 initiatives may receive the bulk of resources to ensure ongoing operations and profitability, while Horizon 2 and 3 initiatives receive sufficient funding to support future growth and innovation.

In summary, McKinsey's Three Horizons Framework is valuable for strategic planning, innovation management, product development, and resource allocation. Its flexibility and adaptability make it suitable for various contexts and scenarios, empowering you to prepare your organization to navigate uncertainty and drive sustainable growth.

How to Use

The Three Horizons Framework strategically guides growth across three phases:

Horizon 1: Maintain and Defend Core Business: The initial phase optimizes existing products and services through enhancements such as upgrades and additional offerings. Goals include margin improvement, process refinement, and a short-term profit boost.

Horizon 2: Nurture Emerging Business: This phase extends offerings into new revenue realms, responding to market shifts and exploring innovations. Initiatives, like new product lines, may involve initial costs but align with the existing business model.

Horizon 3: Create Genuinely New Business: The distant horizon focuses on long-term goals, strategic investments, and growth opportunities, with implications for the organization's competitive landscape.

Implementing the framework follows the 70/20/10 rule:

- **70 percent (Horizon 1):** Enhance existing products and services for short-term gains in Horizon 1.
- **20 percent (Horizon 2):** Pursue "bridging" opportunities for extended offerings, acknowledging potential failures in Horizon 2.
- **10 percent (Horizon 3):** Essential for preventing losing focus on ultimate goals amid Horizon 2 complexities.

This balanced allocation ensures strategic progression, avoiding perpetual Horizon 2 activities and guiding the organization through each growth horizon.

Notes for Your Use

- **Gather Information:** Gather data on the organization's current state, including existing products and sectors, emerging opportunities, and potential growth areas over different time horizons.
- **Evaluate:** Discuss the organization's strategic position and growth potential across three horizons. Analyze the performance of existing products/services, identify emerging trends, and evaluate disruptive innovations that could shape the future landscape.
- **Connect:** Understand how initiatives in each horizon contribute to overall growth objectives and align with the organization's long-term vision.

- **Develop Strategy:** Develop strategies tailored to each horizon, balancing short-term optimization with long-term innovation.
- **Implement Strategy:** Implement strategic initiatives according to the 70/20/10 rule, allocating resources proportionally across the three horizons.

Characteristic Checklist

Similar to the first section, the last model in the second section is a straightforward checklist that you and your team should utilize when finalizing the evaluation of Characteristics in your situation analysis. The provided table serves as a guide, organizing the discussion and providing links to content within the second "C" of the toolbox. While the questions in the Characteristics section primarily focus on the products or services your company offers customers, many of these tools can also be applied to assess business units or other elements of your organization at a broader level.

Model 18 of 50: Characteristics Checklist

Question	Tools	Your team's thoughts
What are we offering customers?	Kotler 5 Product Levels	
Where are our products and services in their evolution?	Diffusion of Innovation Product life cycle	
What are the vital few?	Pareto Analysis	
Are we clear on our break-even?	Break-even analysis	
Do we have a resilient portfolio, or can we create resiliency?	McKinsey 3 Horizons BCG Growth-Share matrix	

SECTION 3

Customers and Collaborators: Increasing Inferential Knowledge with Less Control

Assess your customers' strategy against those who value your offer the most.

The Customer and Collaborator band evaluates the alignment between your offerings and evolving customer needs. This phase involves deeply exploring distinct customer segments and the value they derive from your offerings. Within this dimension, you cultivate a thorough understanding of which customer segments truly resonate with and appreciate your products or services and how the future may change.

Each model within this "C" provides a method to evaluate the customers and collaborators for whom you created the Characteristics in the prior section. This section delves into the customers and understanding why they buy (or what issues customers use your product or services to solve), what customers value, how customers are similar, how customers create value for you, and when to engage with collaborators to reach customers across the routes to market. Every model in this section leads toward clarity in who to focus your strategy upon. As with all sections, it culminates with a checklist tool designed to facilitate group discussions.

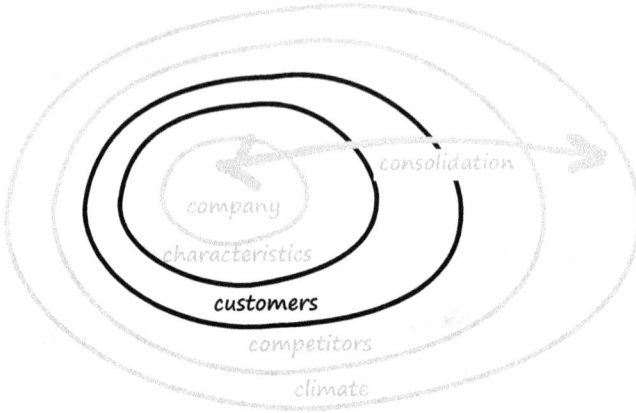

Quick exercise with your team:

Start your Customer and Collaborators assessment as you did in the prior section. Conduct leadership interviews or a leadership workshop, and ask a few simple questions to understand your organization's starting point.

Questions:

- *How are we helping customers with jobs or solutions?*
- *What are the customers' needs or pain points?*
- *How are our customers similar or dissimilar? What are our segments?*
- *What is the value of a customer? How do we calculate this value?*
- *Who are the other essential parties (collaborators) we must rely upon?*
- *How are we aligned with other parties? Who is most and least aligned?*

Jobs-to-Be-Done (Outcome-Driven Innovation)

Brief History

The Jobs-to-Be-Done model originated from the intersection of several key ideas in innovation, marketing, and business strategy, with significant contributions from Clayton Christensen and Anthony Ulwick. Christensen's book, *The Innovator's Solution* (2003), coauthored with Michael Raynor, and later works like *Competing Against Luck* (2016), delve deeply into the Jobs-to-Be-Done framework.[24,25] Ulwick's book, *What Customers Want: Using Outcome-Driven Innovation to Create Breakthrough Products and Service* (2005), was pivotal in elaborating on outcome-driven innovation methodology, which serves as a foundation for the Jobs-to-Be-Done principles.[26] Both Jobs-to-Be-Done and Outcome-Driven Innovation focus on the functional, emotional, and social dimensions of customer needs from a solution perspective.

Model 19 of 50: Jobs-to-Be-Done Table

Who are your current targeted users?	What product, service, or idea do you currently offer?	What is the underlying function of your offer?	What other tools are used with your offer?	What is the core job function or solution the customer wants?
List the groups of customers that you have been targeting. Who isn't using that you thought was?	What workarounds have customers put into place? What are customers trying to avoid?	What is the job that the customer is trying to accomplish?	How do adjacent offers support your offer? What is the primary solution customers seek?	How can you streamline the customer solution (job)? Do new customer segments appear?

When to Use—Understanding the Customer's Fundamental Needs

The Jobs-to-Be-Done theory is a product development approach centered on understanding a customer's specific goal/solution or "job" and the decision-making process that prompts them to "hire" a product to fulfill that job. When applying this framework, the focus is on uncovering the objectives or accomplishments that users seek when purchasing the product, with less emphasis on the product itself. The product then becomes an output of the discussion.

Context and Scenario to Use

The Jobs-to-Be-Done theory offers a profound shift in understanding consumer behavior. It suggests that customers "hire" products or services to fulfill specific jobs or tasks, focusing on the desired outcomes rather than product features. This theory finds application across various business contexts.

- **Product Development and Innovation:** Jobs-to-Be-Done helps prioritize features that directly address customers' needs. For example, a software company developing a productivity tool might focus on time-management features because users hire the tool to boost productivity and reduce stress.
- **Market Segmentation and Targeting:** Jobs-to-Be-Done refines segmentation based on solutions rather than demographics. For instance, a beverage company might target consumers looking for an energy boost instead of focusing on age or profession.
- **Improving Customer Experience:** By recognizing customers' underlying motivations, companies can tailor their offerings to match customer needs better. For example, a hotel chain might focus on amenities that provide business travelers with a restful night and a productive morning.
- **Competitive Strategy:** Jobs-to-Be-Done helps differentiate by addressing unmet needs or solving pain points better than competitors. For example, a streaming service could enhance its recommendation algorithm to help users discover enjoyable content quickly.
- **Marketing and Messaging:** Jobs-to-Be-Done improves messaging by resonating with customers' real needs and desires. A cosmetics brand, for example, might emphasize confidence-building rather than just product features.

In all, the Jobs-to-Be-Done framework enhances the understanding and fulfillment of customer needs, leading to better solutions, increased satisfaction, and a competitive edge.

How to Use

The Jobs-to-Be-Done approach is a versatile business strategy applicable to various products and industries. The Jobs-to-Be-Done serves as a valuable tool for framing the market perspective. Steps to utilize include:

1. **Identify user groups:**
   - Determine the individuals actively using your product, service, or idea.
   - Where do you see nonconsumption? What customers aren't engaged?
   - Classify these users under an overarching term that encapsulates all categories of people employing the product to accomplish a specific job. What are their circumstances?
2. **Identify the current use of your products:**
   - What product, service, or idea do you currently offer?
   - What workarounds are customers putting in place today to change your offer?
   - What tasks are customers trying to avoid?
   - What surprising uses of your product are customers inventing?
3. **Identify the future user group and job:**
   - View the market from the perspective of the job executor, understanding the fundamental functional job they articulate as their primary goal.
     - Do you have the correct user group for your product?
     - What experience are they trying to create?
   - Define the primary job that your user group is attempting to accomplish with your product. Keep the solution in mind.
     - What is your user group trying to accomplish?
     - Explore other products that users typically use in conjunction with yours to fulfill their needs.

The Jobs-to-Be-Done theory facilitates a deeper understanding of your market by shifting the focus from the product to the job users intend to achieve. You can refine your organization's market definition by identifying user groups and discerning the specific jobs they aim to accomplish, enabling more targeted and effective product development or innovation.

This approach prompts you to align your organization's strategies with their customers' genuine needs and objectives, fostering a market-centric perspective that enhances the likelihood of successful product offerings and innovations.

Notes for Your Use

- **Gather Information:** Research customer needs via interviews, surveys, and market analysis to understand the jobs customers want to get done.
- **Evaluate:** Analyze and prioritize these jobs, conducting a Pareto analysis to identify the most critical ones and compare competitor performance.
- **Connect:** Assess if resources and cash generation align with the importance of the jobs addressed by your products.
- **Develop Strategy:** Innovate or enhance products based on critical jobs, considering the product life cycle stage.
- **Implement Strategy:** Continuously adjust the product portfolio, aligning with frameworks like McKinsey's Three Horizons for balance and long-term growth.

Hierarchy of Needs (Value Pyramid)

Brief History

The Hierarchy of Needs, introduced by psychologist Abraham Maslow in 1943, identifies fundamental human motivations, from basic necessities to higher-order desires like self-esteem and altruism.[27] Eric Almquist, John Senior, and Nicolas Bloch later conducted research to identify 30 elements of value or fundamental attributes across four needs levels in the business-to-consumer (B2C).[28] Almquist, with Jamie Cleghorn and

Lori Sherer, later expanded this to business-to-business (B2B) and identified 36 discrete sources of value across five need groups.[29] These frameworks link Maslow's hierarchy of needs to the applicable business context.

Model 20 of 50: Customer Hierarchy of Needs

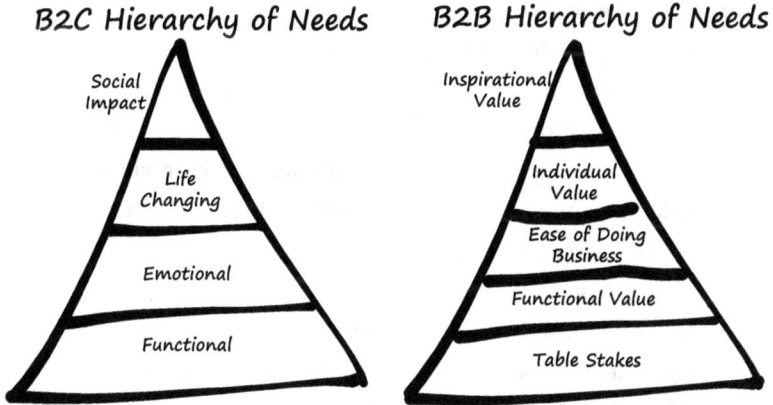

B2C Hierarchy of Needs   ## B2B Hierarchy of Needs

Social Impact
Life Changing
Emotional
Functional

Inspirational Value
Individual Value
Ease of Doing Business
Functional Value
Table Stakes

When to Use—Understanding the Customer's Seriatim of Needs

Customer Hierarchy of Needs helps identify and address unmet needs, tailoring offerings to resonate with different levels of customer requirements. This approach ensures fundamental needs are met first, progressing to higher-level emotional and psychological needs, leading to greater customer satisfaction and loyalty. By understanding and targeting specific customer needs, businesses can differentiate themselves from competitors and build stronger brand connections.

Context and Scenario to Use

The Customer Hierarchy of Needs helps businesses prioritize customer requirements from basic to advanced levels. This framework enhances product development, customer experience, market segmentation, brand positioning, and competitive strategy.

- **Product Development and Innovation:** Companies aim to create products that resonate deeply with customers and meet their evolving needs. For instance, a car manufacturer starts by ensuring basic safety and functionality (basic needs), then enhances comfort and convenience features (performance needs), and finally adds luxury and personalized options to appeal to customers' desires for status and individuality (self-expressive needs).

- **Customer Experience and Service Design:** Businesses strive to provide a comprehensive and satisfying customer experience. An online retailer, for example, ensures that the purchasing process is easy and secure (a basic need), offers fast and reliable shipping (a performance need), and provides excellent customer service with personalized recommendations (an emotional need), ultimately fostering customer loyalty and advocacy (a self-expressive need).

- **Market Segmentation and Targeting:** Effective market segmentation goes beyond demographics to understand deeper customer motivations. A tech company, for instance, segments its market based on customer needs, recognizing that some users prioritize affordability and basic functionality (basic needs), others seek high performance and advanced features (performance needs), and another group values brand prestige and cutting-edge innovation (self-expressive needs).

- **Brand Positioning and Messaging:** It is crucial to craft compelling marketing messages that resonate with different levels of customer needs. For example, a smartphone brand might position its entry-level model by focusing on reliability and affordability (basic needs), its mid-range model by emphasizing performance and camera quality (performance needs), and its premium model by highlighting exclusivity and design (self-expressive needs).

- **Customer Retention and Loyalty Programs:** Retaining customers involves continuously meeting and exceeding their needs. For example, a subscription service ensures uninterrupted access and ease of use (basic needs), enhances the service with personalized content (performance needs), and builds a community with exclusive events and recognition for loyal members (self-expressive needs).

Understanding the Customer Hierarchy of Needs allows you to develop strategies that address functional requirements and build emotional connections, leading to greater customer satisfaction and loyalty. This comprehensive approach ensures sustainable engagement and competitive advantage.

How to Use

To effectively use the Customer Hierarchy of Needs, begin by acknowledging the foundational importance of understanding customers' needs for your product. Jobs-to-Be-Done can be helpful here. The model provides valuable starting points, but the foundational is understanding the customer. To assess a customer's hierarchy of needs, follow these steps:

1. **Identify Key Needs:** Identify the fundamental needs your product or service addresses. Consider basic needs like functionality and reliability, then progress to higher-level needs such as emotional and self-fulfillment aspects.
2. **Conduct Customer Research:** Utilize various research methods, including surveys, interviews, and focus groups, to gather data on customer preferences, behaviors, and motivations. Ask open-ended questions to uncover deeper insights.
3. **Categorize Needs:** Organize the collected data into categories reflecting different hierarchy levels. These typically range from basic needs (e.g., product functionality) to higher-order needs (e.g., brand loyalty and emotional connection).
4. **Prioritize Needs:** Determine the relative importance of each need category to your customers. Analyze the data to identify the most critical needs for their satisfaction and decision-making processes.
5. **Create Customer Profiles:** Develop detailed profiles or personas representing customer segments. Each profile should highlight the specific needs and priorities of that segment.
6. **Map the Hierarchy:** Visualize the hierarchy of needs for each customer segment. Use a pyramid or similar model to illustrate the progression from basic to higher-order needs.

7. **Evaluate Emotional Elements:** Pay special attention to emotional and subjective needs, especially those at higher levels of the hierarchy. Consider using sentiment analysis or qualitative research methods to assess these elements.

8. **Analyze Competitor Offerings:** Compare your findings with competitor offerings to understand how well they meet these needs. Identify gaps and opportunities for differentiation.

9. **Align Strategies:** Align your product development, marketing, and customer service strategies with the identified hierarchy of needs. Ensure that your offerings effectively address the most critical needs.

By following these steps, you can effectively utilize the Customer Hierarchy of Needs to tailor your offerings to customer priorities and meaningfully differentiate your products or services.

Notes for Your Use

- **Gather Information:** Collect customer data through surveys and market research to identify basic, psychological, and self-fulfillment needs. Analyze market trends and competitor offerings to assess gaps in meeting these needs.

- **Evaluate:** Using Pareto analysis, categorize and prioritize customer needs, focusing on those with the highest impact. Then, compare how well current products fulfill these needs relative to competitors' products.

- **Connect:** Align resource allocation with the importance of addressing each level of customer needs. Measure customer satisfaction and loyalty resulting from effectively meeting these needs.

- **Develop Strategy:** Enhance products to better fulfill basic, psychological, and self-fulfillment needs. Develop strategies based on the product life cycle stage and customer feedback.

- **Implement Strategy:** Manage the product portfolio to ensure all levels of customer needs are addressed. Use ongoing customer feedback to refine strategies and maintain alignment with evolving market demands.

Value Proposition Canvas

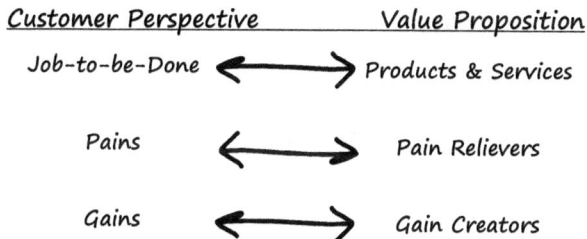

Brief History

The Value Proposition Canvas is a business model tool developed by Alexander Osterwalder, Yves Pigneur, Alan Smith, and Gregory Bernarda in their 2014 book *Value Proposition Design: How to Create Products and Services Customers Want.*[30] The core purpose of the Value Proposition Canvas is to facilitate the strategic alignment between a company's value proposition (the products and services it offers) and the specific needs, pains, and gains of its target customer segments. It provides a structured framework to deeply understand the customer profile and then design the value proposition to fit those customer needs seamlessly.

Model 21 of 50: Value Proposition Canvas
Value Proposition Canvas

Customer Perspective	Value Proposition
Job-to-be-Done ⟷	Products & Services
Pains ⟷	Pain Relievers
Gains ⟷	Gain Creators

When to Use—Linking the Customer Pains and Gains to Your Offerings

The Value Proposition Canvas is a strategic tool for aligning the product or service with the customer's perspective of gains, pains, and jobs. It comprises two sets of linked variables—Value Proposition and Customer Perspective—and centralizes the business model around "What" and "to whom," focusing on how the company delivers value to its customer base. The Client Profile encompasses Jobs-to-Be-Done, Pains, and Gains, while the Value Proposition includes Products and Services, Gain Creators, and Pain Relievers.

Context and Scenario to Use

The Value Proposition Canvas is a strategic tool to align products and services with customer needs, enhancing product development, customer experience, market segmentation, marketing, competitive strategy, and customer retention. A few areas of application include:

- **Product Development and Innovation:** Companies must develop products that solve real customer problems. For instance, a start-up creating a fitness app uses the canvas to identify that users want quick, engaging workouts. Those are the customer gains. Consequently, the app features high-intensity, gamified workouts. Those are the gain creators your offer supports.

- **Customer Experience Improvement:** Businesses aim to enhance satisfaction by understanding customer needs and pain points. For example, a bank uses the canvas to discover customers' frustration with complex fund transfers. This is the pain. They simplify the process and improve the mobile interface, boosting user satisfaction. These are the pain relievers your offer supports.

- **Market Segmentation and Targeting:** Accurate market segmentation helps tailor offerings to different groups. A fashion retailer uses the canvas to segment its market into young adults seeking trendy fashion and budget-conscious parents looking for practicality, enabling targeted marketing campaigns. The offers align with different pains and gains.

- **Marketing and Messaging:** Effective marketing requires resonant messages. An eco-friendly household products company identifies through the canvas that customers value sustainability and cost-effectiveness. Their marketing highlights long-term savings and environmental benefits, appealing to eco-conscious consumers. They link the gains that their product creates to the specific customer segment.

- **Customer Retention and Loyalty Programs**—Retaining customers requires understanding their evolving needs. An e-commerce platform uses the canvas to identify that loyal customers appreciate personalized recommendations and fast shipping. They create a loyalty program offering these perks, increasing retention and repeat purchases.

By focusing on customer pains, gains, and Jobs-to-Be-Done, the Value Proposition Canvas helps you create products and services that drive satisfaction and competitive advantage by developing product offerings that include pain relievers and gain creators.

How to Use

The Value Proposition Canvas is a comprehensive tool that amalgamates key elements to ensure your product or service aligns seamlessly with customer needs. Here's a step-by-step guide to effectively use the canvas:

1. **The Customers:** Identify your prospective customers. Determine the segment of customers you intend to target or have been targeting. Know who you plan to sell to.
2. **The Job:**
   - Identify the Jobs-to-Be-Done. Distinguish between job types:
     - Functional jobs: Perform or complete a specific task.
     - Social jobs: Enhance social status or look good.
     - Personal/emotional jobs: Appeal to emotional status or feelings.
   - Consider the context in which the customer performs the job or interacts with the product or service.
   - Assess the importance of the job to the customer.
3. **The Pains:** Seek to understand what annoys your customer about the job in context. These usually fall into the following groupings:
   - Undesired outcomes, problems, or characteristics.
   - Obstacles to completion.
4. **The Gains:** Understand what the customer truly desires as an outcome. These usually follow this hierarchy:
   - Required gains: Basic must-haves.
   - Expected gains: Not required but usual in the market.
   - Desired gains: Beyond expected, typically not in the market.
   - Unexpected gains: Beyond customer expectations.

5. **Rank the Jobs-to-Be-Done, Pains, and Gains:** Understand what impacts your customer in context by ranking these elements.

6. **Products and Services:**
   - List your offer to the selected customer segment and consider the following:
     - Physical/tangible features.
     - Intangible elements of your service.
   - Assess the relevance of each to your customers from the Jobs-to-Be-Done perspective.

7. **The Pain Relievers:** List how your product or service alleviates customer pains. You may not address all pains, but ensure you assess the most significant ones.

8. **The Gain Creators:** List how your product or service creates customer gains. Address the most critical gains first.

9. **Design Your Fit:** Determine how to adjust your pain relievers and gain creators to best align with the gains and pains of your targeted customer segment. Consider how this varies across your different customer segments.

By following these steps, the Value Proposition Canvas becomes a powerful tool for refining your product or service to meet customer expectations and enhance its market fit.

Notes for Your Use

- **Gather Information:** Through research and interviews, collect customer insights on pains (frustrations, obstacles) and gains (desired outcomes, benefits). Understand your product or service's features and unique selling points.
- **Evaluate:** Identify customer jobs, pains related to these jobs, and desired gains. Analyze how your offering addresses these pains and delivers gains compared to competitors.
- **Connect:** Ensure alignment between customer needs and your value propositions. Evaluate resource allocation to support effective value delivery.

- **Develop Strategy:** Enhance existing value propositions or create new ones based on identified customer needs and competitive differentiation.
- **Implement Strategy:** Execute plans to communicate and deliver your value propositions effectively. Monitor customer feedback and market changes to optimize your offerings continuously.

4 Cs of Inter-company Collaboration

Brief History

The 4 Cs of Inter-company Collaboration is a conceptual framework created by Simon Reese in *Inter-Company Interaction Framework: Understanding the 4 Cs Framework to Promote Learning.*[31] It helps members of an inter-company structure understand each partner company's interest in collaborating toward joint objectives. The framework emphasizes the importance of consistent knowledge sharing and identifying interaction patterns to prevent misalignment and ensure a shared vision.

Model 22 of 50: Reese's 4 Cs of Inter-company Collaboration

Reese 4C of Inter-company Collaboration

Collaborating: sacrificing to improve the capabilities of the partner and team

Cooperate: sacrificing specific resources to support your success

Coordinate: aligning sequential activities to support success

Communicate: base interaction, simple sharing of information

When to Use—Assessing the Collaboration Toward a Shared Vision

Use the 4 Cs of the Inter-company Collaboration framework when interactions across collaborating companies need alignment toward a shared vision. Misalignment can hinder delivering a cohesive product message to the end consumer in a marketplace where the route-to-market involves multiple partners. The 4 Cs framework, based on learning models, helps understand and address these interactions, promoting progressive patterns of integration that enhance collaboration. Each of the 4 Cs has a different rationale for why the parties interact. By employing the 4 Cs, companies can improve interaction and ensure that all partners are working toward common objectives, leading to a more unified and effective market approach.

Context and Scenario to Use

The 4 Cs framework (Communication, Coordination, Cooperation, and Collaboration) is highly beneficial in various sales and marketing contexts, promoting alignment and enhancing effectiveness. Here are some specific scenarios:

- **Strategic Partnerships:** When companies form alliances to co-market or co-sell products, the 4 Cs framework ensures clear communication of goals, coordinated marketing strategies, cooperative resource sharing, and collaborative campaign execution. The framework aids in assessing where along the 4 Cs the two companies are interacting and whether the levels are similar, facilitating smoother partnerships and aligned strategies.
- **Channel Management:** For businesses that rely on distribution channels, using the 4 Cs helps align channel partners with the company's marketing objectives. This ensures consistent messaging and collaborative efforts to maximize reach and effectiveness across both organizations. This alignment fosters stronger partnerships and more effective market penetration.
- **Product Launches:** During a new product's launch, the 4 Cs framework helps ensure that all external stakeholders are aligned and collaborating toward the same vision of success. Clear communication and coordination among partners,

suppliers, and distributors maximize the impact and ensure a cohesive market approach, leading to a more successful product introduction.

- **Market Expansion:** When entering new markets, the 4 Cs framework helps align different external partners, ensuring resources are shared effectively to penetrate the market successfully. Coordinated efforts and cooperative strategies among partners can help overcome market entry barriers and achieve faster growth.

Using the 4 Cs framework, you can assess partner alignment toward shared objectives. Misalignment across the Cs often leads to conflict, so understanding the stage at which both parties operate is crucial. The framework facilitates the identification of potential gaps in interaction levels, allowing for targeted improvements. This understanding leads to more effective sales and marketing strategies and enhanced overall performance. The 4 Cs framework promotes a structured approach to evaluating interactions, ensuring that all parties work toward common goals and achieve mutual success.

How to Use

To effectively use the 4 Cs framework (Communication, Coordination, Cooperation, and Collaboration), follow these steps:

1. **Communication:** Establish transparent and open channels for sharing information across parties.
   - **Identify Stakeholders:** Determine who needs to be informed and involved.
   - **Set Communication Channels:** Choose appropriate platforms (e.g., e-mails, meetings, project management tools).
   - **Establish Frequency:** Decide how often updates and communications should occur.
   - **Ensure Clarity:** Communicate goals, expectations, and progress clearly to all stakeholders.

- ○ **Understand Limitations:** Do not expect to receive deep engagement alignment in the communication stage. This is the starting point.
- ○ **Understand Partners:** Why does the partner seek the information?

2. **Coordination:** Align activities and resources across parties.
   - ○ **Define Roles:** Clarify each partner's roles and tasks.
   - ○ **Align Activities:** Ensure that both partners understand activities.
   - ○ **Develop a Timeline:** Create a project timeline with key milestones.
   - ○ **Monitor Progress:** Use tools and methods to track progress and address any issues promptly.
   - ○ **Understand limitations:** Do not expect the partner to interact beyond the activities outlined in the partnership and expect a short-term focus.
   - ○ **Understand Partners:** What success is the partner gaining from the aligned activities?

3. **Cooperation:** Align common effort and sacrifice of specific resources across parties to meet a task.
   - ○ **Build Trust:** Develop trust through transparency and reliability.
   - ○ **Encourage Mutual Support:** Promote a culture of helping and supporting each partner's efforts.
   - ○ **Address Conflicts:** Establish conflict resolution mechanisms to handle disagreements constructively.
   - ○ **Share Resources:** Encourage sharing resources toward the system's long-term benefit (both partners).
   - ○ **Understand Limitations:** Do not expect the partner to align fully on the long-term goals.
   - ○ **Understand Partners:** What are the partners' long-term goals?

4. **Collaboration:** Work together toward common goals and objectives to improve all parties' capabilities.
   - ○ **Joint Planning:** Involve all partners in planning to ensure shared ownership and commitment.
   - ○ **Integrated Efforts:** Ensure all activities are integrated and aligned with the common goal.

- ○ **Innovative Solutions:** Leverage collective creativity to find innovative solutions.
- ○ **Evaluate and Adapt:** Regularly review collaborative efforts and adapt strategies to improve outcomes.
- ○ **Understand Limitations:** None as long as the parties remain aligned.
- ○ **Understand Partners:** How are the partner's long-term goals being met with the inter-company collaboration?

By systematically applying the 4 Cs framework, you can enhance your organization's inter-company collaborations, leading to more effective partnerships and successful joint initiatives. This structured approach ensures that all parties are aligned and working cohesively toward shared objectives.

Notes for Your Use

- **Gather Information:** Identify the specific collaboration context, such as strategic partnerships, channel management, product launches, or market expansion. Collect data on partners' roles, goals, and resources.
- **Evaluate:** Assess each partner's communication, coordination, cooperation, and collaboration capabilities. Determine their current alignment and identify areas needing improvement.
- **Connect:** Identify shared goals and potential conflicts. Analyze how well each partner's activities, resources, and long-term objectives align with the collaboration framework.
- **Develop Strategy:** Create strategies to enhance communication, coordination, cooperation, and collaboration. Focus on joint planning and integrated efforts for both partners and encourage trust-building and resource sharing.
- **Implement Strategy:** Apply the developed strategies, ensuring clear communication and coordinated activities. Regularly monitor progress, adjust as needed, and review collaborative efforts to optimize outcomes.

Segment–Target–Position (STP)

Brief History

STP (Segmentation, Targeting, Positioning) emerged from the evolution of marketing thought in the mid-20th century. While Wendell Smith introduced market segmentation in 1956, challenging mass marketing approaches, the concept of targeting developed in the 1970s as companies recognized the need to focus resources on specific segments.[32] Ries and Trout introduced positioning in *The Positioning Era Cometh*.[33] They later expanded the concept in their book, *Positioning: The Battle for Your Mind*.[34] Philip Kotler then unified these concepts into the cohesive STP framework.

Model 23 of 50: Segment–Target–Position (STP) Model

Segment-Target-Position

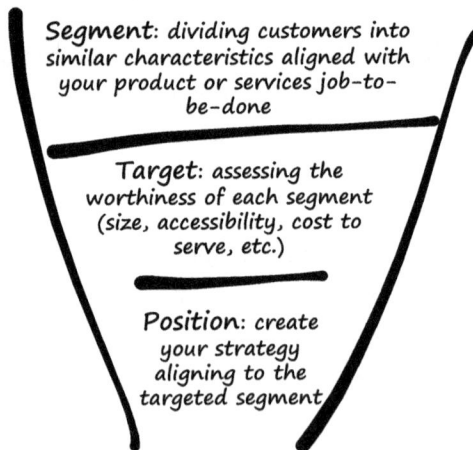

Segment: dividing customers into similar characteristics aligned with your product or services job-to-be-done

Target: assessing the worthiness of each segment (size, accessibility, cost to serve, etc.)

Position: create your strategy aligning to the targeted segment

When to Use—Refine Your Customer Offer

The STP marketing model is a streamlined and efficient approach widely utilized in modern marketing to focus limited positioning resources on a few targeted customer segments. It entails identifying valuable customer segments through targeting and tailoring unique marketing strategies for each. Advancements in marketing technology enhance the precision of STP, contributing to improved business effectiveness. Consider this approach most when looking for efficiency in existing offers through focusing resources.

Context and Scenario of Use

Kotler's STP model is a marketing framework that helps businesses identify and serve the most lucrative market segments, tailor marketing strategies, and position their offerings effectively. A few examples include:

1. **Consumer Electronics Company**
   - Segmentation: The company divides its market into tech enthusiasts, budget-conscious consumers, and business professionals.
   - Targeting: They focus on tech enthusiasts and business professionals by developing high-performance gadgets with the latest features for enthusiasts and reliable, productivity-enhancing devices for professionals.
   - Positioning: High-end advertising and partnerships with tech influencers position their products as the pinnacle of innovation and efficiency, thereby lining up with the targeted segment.
2. **Automotive Industry**
   - Segmentation: A car manufacturer identifies segments such as eco-conscious drivers, luxury seekers, and families.
   - Targeting: They target eco-conscious drivers with electric vehicles and families with spacious, safe cars.
   - Positioning: Marketing campaigns emphasize the environmental benefits of electric cars and the safety features of family cars, positioning them as leaders in sustainability and family safety, which links to the targeted segments.
3. **Fashion Retailer**
   - Segmentation: The retailer segments its market into fast-fashion consumers, luxury shoppers, and eco-friendly buyers.
   - Targeting: They target each segment with specific product lines: trendy, affordable clothes for fast-fashion consumers, high-end designer collections for luxury shoppers, and sustainable garments for eco-friendly buyers.

- ○ Positioning: Through differentiated advertising campaigns and store designs, they position their brands uniquely within each segment, from affordable fashion to luxury and sustainability.

4. **Beverage Company**
   - ○ Segmentation: The company identifies segments such as health-conscious individuals, young adults, and athletes.
   - ○ Targeting: They target health-conscious individuals with organic, low-sugar drinks and young adults with trendy, flavored beverages marketed through social media influencers.
   - ○ Positioning: Their products are positioned as the healthiest and trendiest options on the market, backed by endorsements from nutritionists and influencers.

5. **Hospitality Industry**
   - ○ Segmentation: A hotel chain segments its customers into business travelers, vacationers, and budget travelers.
   - ○ Targeting: They target business travelers with amenities like high-speed Internet and conference rooms, as well as vacationers with luxury spa services and family-friendly activities.
   - ○ Positioning: Hotels are positioned as the best choice for business efficiency and leisure luxury, with tailored messaging for each target group.

By applying Kotler's STP model, you can effectively identify, reach, and serve your organization's target markets by ensuring that their offerings meet specific customer needs and preferences, leading to improved market performance and competitive advantage.

How to Use

Using the STP model involves a strategic approach to meet the diverse needs of customers. Here's a concise guide on employing the STP model:

1. **Segmentation:** To effectively cater to various customer needs, start with market segmentation. This involves dividing customers into groups based on common characteristics and needs. To tailor your approach to each group, utilize various segmentation criteria, such as demographic, geographic, psychographic, and behavioral factors.

2. **Targeting:** Once you've identified audience segments, move on to targeting. Assess the worthiness of each segment for marketing efforts by considering factors like potential customer size, profitability, measurability, accessibility, and your company's ability to serve the segment. Select the segments that align with your business goals and capabilities.

3. **Positioning:** Determine your product's functional positioning strategy to target valuable customer segments effectively. Choose an appropriate marketing mix for each segment. Enhance your product's positioning by identifying its unique selling points and creating a positioning map to understand how different segments perceive it. Highlight distinctive advantages over competitors and communicate these effectively through a clear value proposition in your marketing campaign.

By systematically implementing STP, you can tailor your organization's marketing strategies to diverse customer segments and gain a competitive edge over those using a universal approach.

Notes for Your Use

- **Gather Information:** Segment the market by dividing customers based on demographics, geography, psychographics, and behavior.
- **Evaluate:** Assess the attractiveness of each segment, considering factors such as size, profitability, and alignment with your business goals.
- **Connect:** Select and target segments that match your business capabilities and objectives, then develop a tailored marketing mix for each.
- **Develop Strategy:** Formulate a positioning strategy that highlights your product's unique selling points and creates a clear value proposition.
- **Implement Strategy:** Execute your marketing campaign, focusing on differentiated messaging and positioning to resonate with each targeted segment.

Customer Lifetime Value

Brief History

Customer Lifetime Value (CLV) originated in the 1980s as businesses recognized the importance of long-term customer relationships over one-time transactions. Initially used in direct marketing, CLV gained broader adoption in the 1990s with advances in data analytics and customer relationship management (CRM) systems. CLV quantifies the total revenue a customer generates throughout their relationship with a company and includes the cost to acquire, cost to retain, and lifetime purchase.

Model 24 of 50: Customer Lifetime Value

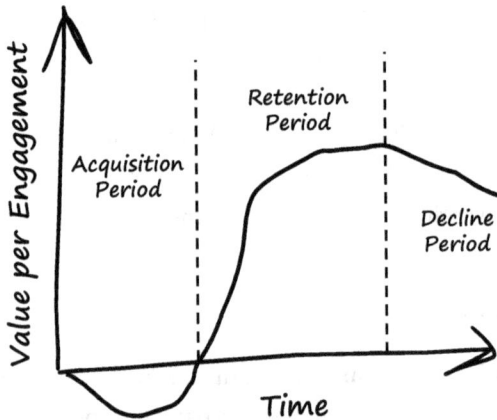

Formula

Customer Lifetime = (Average purchase price –Average cost to serve) X
Value   purchases per year – (customer acquisition cost to
(per year)   gain first purchase + customer retention cost per year)

When to Use—Understanding the Value of Your Customers

CLV calculations are crucial for optimizing marketing strategies, customer retention, product development, and financial planning. CLV calculations help determine optimal marketing spend, target high-value customers, and design effective retention programs. CLV calculations guide product enhancements, cross-selling, and upselling efforts while supporting value-based pricing and strategic discounts.

Additionally, CLV calculations aid in accurate revenue forecasting, investment decisions, and personalized customer engagement. Businesses can enhance customer satisfaction and drive long-term profitability by prioritizing high-CLV customers for premium support. Overall, CLV is essential for making data-driven decisions that maximize customer value and business success.

Context and Scenario to Use

CLV is a pivotal metric in various business contexts, offering insights into customer profitability and informing strategic decisions. Here are key scenarios where CLV is particularly useful:

1. **Marketing Strategy:**
   - Customer Segmentation: CLV helps segment customers based on profitability, allowing businesses to tailor marketing efforts toward high-value segments. For instance, a company might allocate more resources to retain top-tier customers who generate higher CLV.
   - Acquisition Cost Management: By understanding CLV, businesses can determine the maximum amount to spend on acquiring new customers while ensuring profitability. For example, if a customer's CLV is $1,000, the company might set an acquisition cost limit of $200 to maintain a healthy profit margin.
2. **Customer Retention:**
   - Personalized Engagement: CLV guides personalized retention strategies, such as exclusive offers or loyalty programs, aimed at customers with the highest potential value. For example, a retailer might offer VIP discounts or early access to sales to its most valuable customers.
   - Churn Prevention: Monitoring CLV trends can help identify at-risk customers. Businesses can then implement targeted interventions, such as personalized support or special offers, to prevent churn and extend customer relationships.

3. **Product Development and Cross-Selling:**
   - Product Enhancements: CLV insights can inform product development by highlighting the preferences and behaviors of high-value customers. For instance, a software company might prioritize features that are highly valued by its most profitable users.
   - Cross-Selling and Upselling: By analyzing CLV, businesses can identify opportunities for cross-selling and upselling. For example, a telecom company might offer customers with high-CLV bundle packages, increasing their overall spending.
4. **Financial Forecasting:**
   - Revenue Projections: CLV provides a basis for accurate revenue forecasting by estimating future revenue streams from existing customers. This helps in budgeting and financial planning, ensuring resources are allocated effectively.
   - Investment Decisions: Understanding CLV helps make informed investment decisions, such as expanding into new markets or developing new products, by evaluating potential long-term returns from different customer segments.

In summary, CLV is a versatile tool that aids in strategic planning, marketing, customer retention, product development, and financial forecasting. By leveraging CLV, you can optimize your organization's strategies to enhance customer relationships and drive long-term profitability.

How to Use

To effectively use CLV and assess acquisition and retention costs, follow these steps:

1. **Define Customer Segments:** Identify customer segments based on demographics, behavior, or purchase history. Segmenting helps tailor acquisition and retention strategies more precisely.
2. **Calculate Average Value:** Determine the average transaction value per customer by dividing total revenue by the number of purchases

over a specific period. Subtract the cost to serve (CTS) the customer by dividing the total costs by the number of purchases over a particular period.

3. **Determine Purchase Frequency:** Calculate the average number of purchases a customer makes in a specific time frame. This helps in estimating the purchase frequency rate.

4. **Estimate Customer Lifespan:** Estimate how long an average customer continues to buy from your company. This can be derived from historical data on customer retention and churn rates.

5. **Calculate CLV:** Use the formula CLV = (Average Purchase Value) × (Purchase Frequency) × (Customer Lifespan). This provides the average revenue generated from a customer over their entire relationship with your business.

6. **Assess Customer Acquisition Cost (CAC):** Calculate the cost of acquiring a new customer by dividing the total marketing and sales expenses by the number of new customers acquired in a specific period. CAC = Total Acquisition Cost/Number of New Customers.

7. **Evaluate Customer Retention Cost:** Determine the cost of retaining existing customers, including loyalty programs, customer service, and marketing campaigns. Retention Cost = Total Retention Expense/Number of Retained Customers.

8. **Analyze Profitability:** To understand profitability, compare CLV with CAC and retention costs. Ideally, for a sustainable business model, CLV should be significantly higher than CAC.

9. **Optimize Marketing and Retention Strategies:** Use insights from CLV, CAC, and retention costs to refine marketing strategies, focusing on high-value customers and cost-effective acquisition channels. Implement targeted retention programs to enhance customer loyalty and increase CLV.

10. **Monitor and Adjust:** Continuously track and analyze CLV, CAC, and retention metrics. Adjust strategies based on performance data and changing market conditions to maximize customer value and business profitability.

By systematically applying these steps, you can effectively use CLV to make informed decisions about customer acquisition, retention, and overall strategy.

Notes for Your Use

- **Gather Information:** Define customer segments based on demographics, behavior, and purchase history.
- **Evaluate:** Calculate the average transaction value, purchase frequency, and customer lifespan. Use the formula to determine CLV.
- **Connect:** Assess CAC and retention costs to understand overall profitability.
- **Develop Strategy:** Refine marketing and retention strategies based on CLV, CAC, and retention insights to focus on high-value customers and cost-effective methods.
- **Implement Strategy:** Monitor performance, track metrics, and adjust strategies for ongoing optimization.

The Value Stick

Brief History

Felix Oberholzer-Gee introduced the Value Stick in his book *Better, Simpler Strategy*, published in 2021.[35] In this book, Oberholzer-Gee discusses the importance of simplifying business strategy to enhance value creation and capture. The Value Stick is a conceptual framework that illustrates the relationship between customer willingness to pay (WTP) and the willingness to sell (WTS). It helps businesses analyze and optimize how they create and capture value. The model emphasizes that understanding these dynamics is crucial for developing effective strategies that align with customer expectations and improve profitability.

Model 25 of 50: Value Stick

Value Stick

Willingness to Pay = what customers most value and maximum price

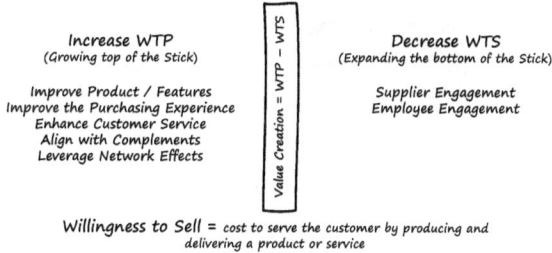

Increase WTP		Decrease WTS
(Growing top of the Stick)		(Expanding the bottom of the Stick)
Improve Product / Features		Supplier Engagement
Improve the Purchasing Experience		Employee Engagement
Enhance Customer Service		
Align with Complements		
Leverage Network Effects		

Value Creation = WTP − WTS

Willingness to Sell = cost to serve the customer by producing and delivering a product or service

When to Use—Understanding How to Increase the Value of Your Customers

The Value Stick approach develops strategies that focus on increasing value by analyzing two opposing sides of the value stick—customer WTP and WTS. It helps organizations align offerings with customer expectations, optimize costs without diminishing perceived value, and enhance competitive positioning. Ideal for product development, market entry, strategic reviews, and cost optimization, the Value Stick enables targeted improvements that boost value creation and capture, ensuring strategic initiatives prioritize high-value opportunities and profitability.

Context and Scenario to Use

By applying the Value Stick, you can systematically enhance your organization's strategic initiatives, align product offerings with customer expectations, and optimize their cost structures, ultimately leading to improved value creation and capture.

- **New Product Development:** Use the Value Stick to assess customer WTP for a new wearable device, evaluate production costs, and enhance features to justify a premium price before launch.

- **Market Entry Analysis:** Apply the Value Stick to analyze local market conditions for a potential new geographic entry. This ensures that customer WTP exceeds the calculated WTS for a profitable market strategy.
- **Competitive Positioning:** Leverage the Value Stick to assess customer preferences and competitor pricing, identify inefficiencies in the cost structure, and enhance perceived value through loyalty programs while optimizing operational costs.
- **Cost Optimization Initiatives:** Use the Value Stick to break down production costs in a manufacturing firm, identify areas for cost reduction, and ensure pricing strategies remain competitive while maintaining customer satisfaction.
- **Innovation Strategies:** Implement the Value Stick to prioritize software feature development by analyzing customer feedback on desired features, assessing associated development costs, and aligning teams on high-value enhancements.

The Value Stick is a powerful tool for organizations seeking to enhance their strategic initiatives. Businesses can better align their offerings with customer expectations, optimize operational efficiencies, and drive innovation by systematically analyzing customer WTP and cost structures.

How to Use

Using the Value Stick involves systematically analyzing and enhancing how a business creates and captures value. Here's a step-by-step guide on how to effectively utilize the Value Stick in your strategic planning:

Step 1: Assess Customer WTP

- Identify Core Value Drivers: Conduct market research to identify what customers value most in your product or service. This could include brand trust, product expertise, or ease of access. Use surveys and focus groups and analyze sales data to pinpoint features that elevate WTP.

- Quantify WTP: Determine the maximum price customers are willing to pay. Gather insights directly from customers or infer from competitor pricing and sales data. Consider ways to increase perceived value, like offering faster delivery, improving in-store experiences, or adding useful complementary services.

Step 2: Evaluate WTS

- Break Down Costs to Serve: Assess all costs involved in producing and delivering your product or service, from fixed costs like overhead to variable expenses like labor and materials. Reducing WTS involves more than cutting costs—it means finding ways to add value for both your company and partners.
- Identify Cost Drivers: Analyze processes impacting WTS. For suppliers, consider costs associated with supply chain logistics and collaboration; for employees, examine conditions impacting satisfaction, such as workplace conditions or opportunities for growth. Both efforts lead to lower WTS through value creation and optimized operations.

Step 3: Calculate Value Created

- Calculate Value Creation: The difference between WTP and WTS is your value created. Maximizing this gap is key: higher WTP and lower WTS increase value.
- Analyze Value Creation: A positive value shows strong value creation, while a negative figure suggests reevaluating either pricing strategy or cost structure. Look for opportunities to close this gap by enhancing WTP or reducing WTS.

Step 4: Identify Opportunities for Enhancement (Extend the Value Stick)

- **Enhance WTP:** Use targeted strategies to raise customer WTP:
  - Product Quality and Features: Boost product quality, user experience, or accessibility. Offering tailored, superior experiences can significantly raise WTP.
  - Create Unique Experiences: Provide value-adding experiences beyond the product itself, like personalized service or in-store brand experiences that create customer delight.
  - Build Complements: Identify complementary products or services to increase WTP. Partner with brands or develop products that make your core offering more appealing while balancing complements that could become substitutes.
  - Leverage Network Effects: Amplify WTP through direct, indirect, or platform-driven network effects. For example, direct effects enhance value for each user as more join, while indirect effects boost perceived value via complementary products or services.
- **Reduce WTS:** Optimizing Supplier and Employee Engagement:
  - Supplier Engagement:
    - Collaborative Cost Reduction: Work closely with suppliers to find shared cost-reduction strategies, such as joint investments in logistics or technology.
    - Transparent Communication and Long-Term Partnerships: Develop trust through open communication, sharing demand forecasts and strategic goals, which can reduce uncertainty and lead suppliers to offer more favorable terms.
    - Supplier Training and Recognition: Invest in supplier training and reward high performance to strengthen partnerships and motivate suppliers to help reduce costs.
  - Employee Engagement:
    - Enhance Workplace Conditions: Create a positive, supportive work environment that boosts job satisfaction. Employees

who feel valued are less likely to require large financial incentives, effectively lowering WTS.

- Offer Training and Career Development: Provide clear paths for growth and skills development, which increase loyalty and engagement, reducing turnover-related costs.
- Empower Employees: Grant autonomy and decision-making power to build a sense of ownership. Engaged employees are often motivated to contribute beyond their roles without additional compensation demands.
- Recognize and Reward Performance: Establish recognition programs for achievements. Rewarding value-creating behaviors drives motivation and productivity.
- Build a Mission-Driven Culture: Align your mission with employee values, fostering a connection to the company that makes employees more invested in its success, even at potentially lower compensation levels.

By systematically applying these steps and focusing on creating value for customers, suppliers, and employees, you can make better strategic decisions, achieve greater operational efficiency, and enhance profitability. This Value Stick approach ensures that value creation and capture are central to your organization's strategic direction.

Notes for Your Use

- **Gather Information:** Assess customer WTP and your WTS/CTS, conducting market research to identify customer preferences and your internal production costs.
- **Evaluate:** Analyze WTP and WTS to determine the value created, identifying inefficiencies in the cost structure and potential areas for enhancing product features or services.
- **Connect:** By understanding market conditions and competitor pricing, align product offerings with customer expectations, ensuring strategies meet customer needs while maintaining profitability.

- **Develop Strategy:** Based on insights gained from the Value Stick analysis, formulate strategies for new product development, market entry, competitive positioning, cost optimization, and innovation.
- **Implement Strategy:** Execute the developed strategies, monitor KPIs, and adjust approaches as needed to continuously enhance value creation and capture.

Customer and Collaborator Checklist

Similar to prior sections, the last model in this third section provides a straightforward checklist for you and your team to use when finalizing the evaluation of customers and collaborators in your situation analysis. This checklist serves as a guide, organizing the discussion and providing links to the models in Section 3. As you discuss the components of the checklist, delve deeply into understanding why customers buy, what they value, how they are similar or dissimilar, with whom you collaborate across the route-to-market, and where you engage with customers to retain value.

First, focus on customer insights. Understand the motivations behind customer purchases, including their primary drivers and what they seek from your product or service. Identify the key values customers place on your offerings: quality, price, convenience, or brand reputation. Assess how customers are similar or dissimilar by segmenting them based on demographics, psychographics, buying behaviors, and needs.

Next, examine your collaborator's insights. Identify who you collaborate with, such as suppliers, distributors, and other partners across the route-to-market. Determine where and how you engage with these collaborators to retain value and ensure effective collaboration. Evaluate the alignment between your goals and those of your collaborators, looking for synergies that can be leveraged for mutual benefit.

By using this checklist and diving deeply into these areas, you can ensure a thorough evaluation of customers and collaborators. This approach will help you make informed decisions and craft strategies that align with customer needs and collaborative goals, ultimately leading to a stronger market position and better business outcomes.

Model 26 of 50: Customer and Collaborator Checklist

Question	Tools	Your team's thoughts
How are we helping customers with jobs or solutions?	Job-to-be-Done Outcome-driven innovation	
What are the customers' needs or pain points?	Value Proposition Hierarchy of Needs	
How are the customers similar or dissimilar?	STP AIDA	
What is the value of our customers?	Customer Lifetime Value Value Stick	
How are we aligned with other parties?	4Cs	

SECTION 4

Competitors: Inferential with Almost No Control

Assess your strategy against the competitor's current strategy and future capabilities.

The Competitor dimension ventures into a realm characterized by diminishing control and increasing ambiguity. At this juncture, the emphasis shifts toward strategically positioning against market rivals by comprehending both their current moves and future intentions. The Competitor band serves as a domain where you discern optimal courses of action and anticipate how others will respond to your initiatives. Each model in this "C" offers a way to distill information about the competitive landscape that your company operates within. Your strategy cannot be created in a vacuum. This section helps you to understand the environment outside your business.

The Competitor section begins with methods to assess the competitive landscape broadly by understanding concentration and growth dynamics. It explores models like competitive concentration analysis and market growth models, which provide insights into how concentrated the market is and which segments are less competitively intense. These models help identify the market structure and pinpoint opportunities or threats.

Next, the models transition to understanding competitor ambitions. This includes analyzing competitors' strategic objectives, strengths and weaknesses, and potential moves. By grouping similar competitors, you can identify clusters within the competitive landscape and strategize interactions and positioning within these clusters. Models such as strategic group analysis and competitor capability profiling are used here to gain deeper insights into your competitors' strategies and predict their future actions.

As with the prior sections, the concluding model is a checklist to aid you in your competitor assessment with your team. This checklist ensures a comprehensive evaluation by covering key areas such as market position, strategic objectives, strengths and weaknesses, and potential future moves of your competitors. By systematically applying this checklist, you can ensure that your competitive analysis is thorough and that your strategies are well-informed and robust.

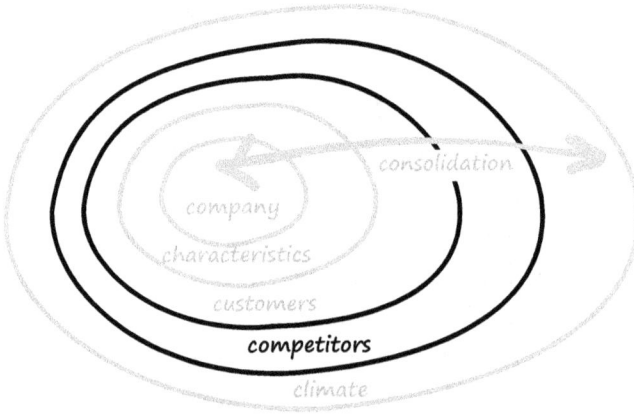

Quick exercise with your team:

Start your competitor assessment the same way you did in the prior sections. Conduct leadership interviews or a leadership workshop, and ask a few simple questions to understand your organization's starting point.

Questions:
- *How competitively intense is our industry? How do we know?*
- *What drives our competitors' actions?*
- *How do we perform versus our competitors? What are our strengths and weaknesses?*
- *What are the competitive groupings and barriers in our industry? How are specific competitors similar?*
- *How are we staying ahead of competitors?*
- *Can we change the competitive structure of our industry via cooperation?*

HHI Index (Competitive Concentration)

Brief History

The Herfindahl–Hirschman Index (HHI), introduced by economist Albert O. Hirschman in 1945, is a metric for assessing market concentration.[36] Employed in pre- and post-M&A scenarios, the HHI gauges competitiveness by measuring company size in relation to industry size. This index plays a pivotal role in business strategy, offering insights into market dynamics and competitive landscapes.

Model 27 of 50: HHI Index
Competitive Market Share

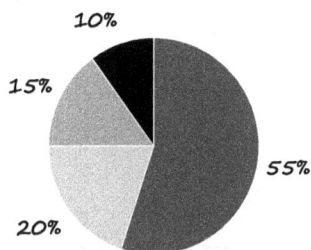

$$HHI = 55^2 + 20^2 + 15^2 + 10^2 = 3,750 \text{ (High Concentration)}$$

Formula

$$HHI = s1^2 + s2^2 + s3^2 + \cdots + sn^2$$

where sn = the market share percentage of firm n expressed as a whole number, not a decimal

- **High** = >2,500
- **Moderate** = 1,500–2,500
- **Low** = <1,500

When to Use—Determine Competitive Concentration in the Market

The HHI is employed in business strategy when assessing market competitiveness. Its simplicity in calculation and minimal data requirements make it advantageous for swiftly gauging market concentration.

Businesses use the HHI to evaluate the competitive landscape, aiding strategic decision making through assessing the industry concentration. Higher concentrations (HHI score) generally indicate high entry barriers and support incumbent strategies. Conversely, lower concentrations generally indicate low entry barriers and support entry strategies.

Context and Scenario to Use

Use HHI to assess market concentration, evaluate competition levels, and effectively inform regulatory decisions, strategic planning, and investment strategies.

- **Antitrust and Competition Policy:** Governments and regulatory bodies worldwide rely on the HHI to gauge market concentration within specific industries. The HHI is a critical tool in assessing whether markets are competitive or if there are risks of monopolistic practices. Regulators use the HHI when evaluating merger proposals between large companies. A high HHI score post-merger indicates reduced competition, which can potentially lead to monopolistic behavior. Regulators intervene to prevent such scenarios to safeguard consumer welfare and ensure fair market practices. By analyzing HHI trends before and after mergers, regulators can make informed decisions that promote competition and prevent anticompetitive behaviors.

- **Strategic Planning and Market Analysis:** Businesses utilize the HHI to analyze market structures and competitive dynamics thoroughly. Understanding the degree of market concentration helps companies assess competitive threats and opportunities for strategic positioning. Companies conduct HHI assessments to identify potential competitive threats and market opportunities when entering new markets or expanding product lines. A low HHI score in a fragmented market may indicate ample market entry. Conversely, a high HHI score suggests a concentrated market where few competitors prevail, requiring strategic differentiation or niche targeting strategies to succeed.

- **Investment and Financial Analysis:** HHI is crucial in investment and financial analysis, providing insights into industry attractiveness and investment risks. Investors and financial analysts use HHI scores to evaluate the competitive landscape and predict industry profitability and growth potential. Equity analysts monitor HHI trends to assess industry stability and growth prospects. A declining HHI score may indicate increasing competition and potential market fragmentation, presenting opportunities for diversified investment strategies. Conversely, a rising HHI score might signal consolidation and reduced competition, influencing investment decisions to mitigate risks associated with monopolistic practices.

In summary, the HHI is a versatile tool for antitrust regulation, strategic planning, and financial analysis. It provides valuable insights that guide regulatory decisions, initiatives, and investment strategies in various industries.

How to Use

The HHI is a simple mathematical formula. To use the HHI, follow these steps:

1. **Gather Market Share Data:** Collect market share data for all firms operating in the market of interest. Each firm's market share represents its proportion of the total market size.
2. **Calculate Squared Market Shares:** Square the market share of each firm. This emphasizes the impact of larger firms in the calculation. Be sure to square the number, not the decimal.
3. **Sum the Squared Market Shares:** Add up all the squared market shares. This cumulative sum is a key component of the HHI calculation.
4. **Interpret the HHI Score:** Evaluate the HHI score obtained. The HHI can range from close to 0 to 10,000.
   - A low HHI (below 1,500) suggests a highly competitive market with numerous firms and low concentration.

- ○ A moderate HHI (between 1,500 and 2,500) indicates moderate concentration, with a mix of dominant and smaller firms.
- ○ A high HHI (above 2,500) signals high concentration, potentially pointing to a market dominated by a few large firms.

5. **Draw Conclusions:** Use the HHI to draw conclusions about market competitiveness. A declining HHI over time may indicate increased competition, while a rising HHI could signal decreased competition or emerging market dominance.

6. **Consider Implications:** Reflect on the implications of the HHI score for business strategy. A high HHI may raise concerns about monopolistic behavior, potentially impacting regulatory scrutiny or strategic decision making in mergers and acquisitions. If your business is an incumbent, high HHI is generally beneficial. Conversely, if your business is attempting to enter a market, high HHI is generally detrimental.

By understanding and interpreting the HHI, you can gain valuable insights into market concentration, competition levels, and potential implications for their strategic planning and decision-making processes.

Notes for Your Use

- **Gather Information:** Collect market share data for all firms in the market.
- **Evaluate:** Square each firm's market share to emphasize the impact of larger firms.
- **Connect:** Sum the squared market shares to compute the HHI.
- **Develop Strategy:** Interpret the HHI score to understand market concentration and competitiveness. Use insights to adjust business strategy, considering whether a high or low HHI is beneficial based on your market position.
- **Implement Strategy:** Monitor HHI trends and reflect on implications for regulatory concerns or strategic decisions, such as mergers and market entry.

Rule of Three and Four

Brief History

Bruce Henderson, in his article "The Rule of Three and Four," proposed that a stable competitive industry would ideally have no more than three significant competitors, achieving equilibrium with market shares in a 4:2:1 ratio, thus making the largest competitor no more than four times the size of the smallest of the three.[37] Subsequent testing showed that industries with this three-generalist configuration yielded a 2.5 percent higher return on assets than those with more competitors. Typically, the largest player in such configurations had 1.5–2.5 times the market share of its nearest rival and 4 times that of the smaller one, aligning closely with Henderson's initial 4:2:1 hypothesis. This hypothesis was validated in "BCG Classic Revisited: The Rule of Three and Four" but with a caveat that few industries are progressing toward this stability.[38]

Model 28 of 50: Rules of Three and Four

Rule of 3 and 4

Competitive market share

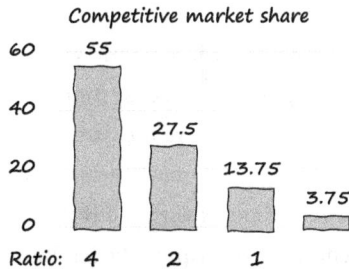

| Ratio: | 4 | 2 | 1 |

When to Use—Evaluate the Competitive Stability in the Market

The Rule of Three and Four is valuable in competitive strategy to understand industry share structure and stability. It highlights that, as markets mature, a consolidation often occurs, leading to a few major players dominating the industry to the point of competitive stability. The gap between these leaders and other players is typically substantial. Significant shifts in market share or industry leadership are uncommon in mature markets with limited market share growth unless prompted by disruptive forces or regulatory changes. Vital to the analysis is that industries with the three generalist structures were the most profitable.

Context and Scenario to Use

Bruce Henderson's Rule of Three and Four is a strategic principle that suggests competitive markets tend to stabilize around three major competitors with relative equilibrium in size across the players, which leaves a small portion of the remaining market for the remaining players. Some common uses are as follows:

- **Market Analysis and Strategy Formulation:** Companies use the Rule of Three and Four to analyze market structures and competitive dynamics. For example, in an industry where the rule applies, businesses may assess the number and strength of competitors to anticipate competitive pressures and plan strategic responses. This analysis helps identify whether the market is consolidating around a few dominant players at equilibrium or has room for additional competitors or growth across competitors.

- **Strategic Planning and Market Entry:** Entrepreneurs and businesses entering new markets or industries apply Henderson's rule to assess competitive intensity and market potential. Before entering a market, a new entrant evaluates whether the market structure aligns with the Rule of Three or Four. This assessment helps determine the feasibility of entering a competitive market or exploring niche opportunities where competition is less intense.

- **Investment and Merger & Acquisition (M&A) Decisions:** Investors and companies considering mergers or acquisitions use the Rule of Three and Four to evaluate market concentration and competitive landscape. When evaluating potential investments or M&A opportunities, stakeholders analyze the market's competitive dynamics based on Henderson's rule. A market conforming to the Rule of Three and Four might signal stability and established players without entry opportunities.

In summary, Bruce Henderson's Rules of Three and Four provides a framework for understanding market competition and stability to guide strategic decisions in market analysis, strategic planning, market entry, and investment evaluations. It helps businesses anticipate competitive behaviors and formulate effective strategies for successfully navigating competitive markets.

How to Use

The Rule of Three and Four is employed by understanding the market share across a defined market. The logic suggests that the optimal equilibrium point occurs when the market share ratio is between any top competitors. Key conditions for this rule include a 4:2:1 ratio in market share among the top three competitors. Beyond the top three, competitors generally hold 0 to 10 percent of the total market share. These conditions are attributed to the stability of competitive markets. Steps to evaluating using the Rule of Three and Four are as follows:

- **Identify Market:** Define the specific market or industry segment you are analyzing.
- **Market Size and Growth:** Assess the market's overall size and growth potential.
- **Competitive Landscape:** Identify all existing competitors and their market shares.
- **Rank Competitors:** Rank competitors based on market share and influence within the market.
- **Identify Top Three Players:** Determine the top three market competitors.
- **Assess the Fourth Player:** Identify if there is a significant fourth player and evaluate their likelihood of surviving long term.
- **Market Share Distribution:** Analyze how market share is distributed among these players and if it aligns with the rule.
- **Adapt Strategy:** If you are not in the top three, consider niche markets or innovative approaches to disrupt the existing hierarchy.

Strategists should shape strategies based on their company's position. The top three players are advised to defend their share or grow aggressively toward the equilibrium point. At the same time, those outside the top three should seek to improve their position through consolidation, shifting the basis of competition, or considering an exit strategy. In mature markets, significant changes in market share are rare, except in cases of disruption or deregulation. Understanding and aligning with these principles can guide effective strategic decisions in the competitive landscape.

Notes for Your Use

- **Gather Information:** Identify the specific market or industry segment and collect data on market size, growth, and existing competitors' market shares.
- **Evaluate:** Rank competitors by market share and influence. Assess if the top three competitors align with the 4:2:1 market share ratio.
- **Connect:** Determine if there is a significant fourth player and analyze their potential for long-term survival.
- **Develop Strategy:** Understand that movement to stability does take time. Generally, in progressing toward equilibrium, the top three players focus on defending or expanding market share. For others, explore niche markets or innovative approaches to improve positioning.
- **Implement Strategy:** Adapt strategies based on your market position and monitor market dynamics to adjust as needed.

Porter's Four Corners

Brief History

Michael Porter first published his Four Corners Analysis in *Competitive Strategy: Techniques for Analyzing Industries and Competitors* in 1980.[39] The Four Corners Model is a strategic framework designed to identify four key elements to gain insights into competitors' motivations and actions and, more importantly, deduce their future ambitions.

Model 29 of 50: Porter's Four Corners

Porter's 4 Corners

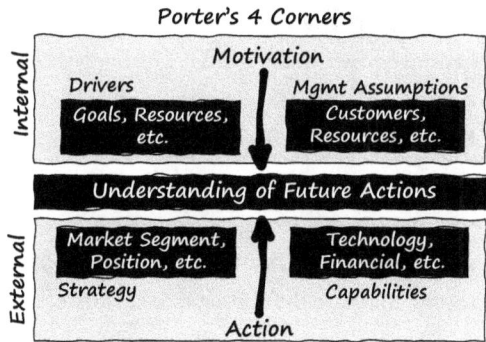

When to Use—Understand Competitor's Motivation

Porter's Four Corners Model analyzes competitors' motivations and actions. Businesses can anticipate competitors' reactions and make informed strategic decisions by examining competitors' internal state (Motivation) and observable actions (Actions), including their drivers, management assumptions, strategy, and capabilities.

Context and Scenario to Use

Porter's Four Corners Analysis is typically used when analyzing competitive dynamics within an industry. Specifically, it helps understand competitors' strategic positioning and behaviors based on their current and potential goals. Here are the main scenarios when Porter's Four Corners Analysis is used:

- **Strategic Planning and Analysis:** Businesses use the Four Corners to assess competitors' strategic intent and goals. This helps them systematically identify objectives such as market share growth, profitability, innovation, or geographic expansion.
- **Competitive Benchmarking:** Organizations compare their strategic goals and positioning against competitors identified through the Four Corners Analysis. This helps identify areas of competitive advantage or vulnerability.
- **Market Entry and Expansion:** Companies use Four Corners to analyze competitors' strategic goals and current actions before

entering a new market or expanding existing operations. This informs market entry strategies and competitive positioning.

- **Mergers and Acquisitions (M&A):** During M&A activities, Four Corners Analysis helps assess the strategic alignment and potential synergies with target companies. It identifies how competitors' strategic goals and capabilities complement or threaten the acquiring firm.

- **Industry Analysis:** Analysts and researchers use Four Corners to analyze and compare the strategic behaviors of competitors within an industry. This analysis provides insights into industry structure, competitive intensity, and profitability potential.

Overall, Porter's Four Corners Analysis is valuable for gaining insights into competitors' strategic objectives and behaviors. It enables you to formulate effective competitive strategies and navigate industry competitive dynamics.

How to Use

Porter's Four Corners Analysis is a strategic framework designed to help you understand your organization's competitors. It examines four key components: Drivers, Management Assumptions, Strategy, and Capabilities. This analysis provides insights into competitors' motivations and actions, enabling firms to develop informed competitive strategies.

Step 1: Identify the Competitor

Select the competitor you wish to analyze. This could be a direct competitor or a company that operates in the same industry but targets different segments.

Step 2: Analyze the Drivers of Competitor Motivation

Examine the factors that drive the competitor's behavior and strategic choices. Consider the following:

- Industry Position: Determine the competitor's market share and position relative to others in the industry.

- Competitor Goals: Identify the competitor's primary objectives, such as growth, market leadership, or profitability.
- Current Strategy: Analyze the strategies currently employed by the competitor.
- Resource Capability: Assess the competitor's financial, human, and technological resources.
- Market Dynamics: Consider external factors impacting the competitor, such as market trends, regulations, and economic conditions.

Step 3: Evaluate Management Assumptions

Understand the beliefs and perceptions of the competitor's leadership that influence decision making. Focus on:

- Understanding of the Competitive Environment: What do they believe about competition in the market?
- Customer Needs and Preferences: How do they perceive customer demands and values?
- Resource Allocation: What assumptions do they make regarding their resources and capabilities?
- Risk Tolerance: What is their approach to risk-taking in strategic decisions?
- Long-Term versus Short-Term Focus: Are they prioritizing immediate results or long-term sustainability?
- Cultural and Ethical Beliefs: How do their values shape their strategies?

Step 4: Examine the Strategy

Analyze the strategic approaches that the competitor employs in the market. Key areas to explore include:

- Competitive Positioning: How does the competitor differentiate itself from others?
- Market Segmentation: What specific customer segments does the competitor target?

- Product Offerings: What products or services do they offer, and how do they innovate?
- Pricing Strategy: What pricing tactics do they use to attract customers?
- Marketing and Promotion: How do they market their products or services?
- Distribution Channels: What channels do they use to reach customers?
- Partnerships and Alliances: Do they have strategic partnerships that enhance their market position?
- Adaptation to Market Trends: How quickly do they respond to emerging trends?

Step 5: Assess Capabilities

Evaluate the skills, resources, and competencies that enable the competitor to execute their strategies effectively. Consider the following:

- Financial Resources: What is their financial health and access to capital?
- Human Resources: How skilled and motivated is their workforce?
- Technological Capabilities: What technology do they leverage for competitive advantage?
- Operational Efficiency: How effective are their supply chain and production processes?
- Brand Strength and Reputation: What is the strength of their brand in the market?
- Intellectual Property: Do they hold valuable patents or proprietary technologies?
- Customer Relationships: How well do they manage customer interactions and loyalty?
- Agility and Adaptability: How quickly can they adjust their strategies in response to market changes?

By systematically analyzing these Four Corners—Drivers, Management Assumptions, Strategy, and Capabilities—you can gain a comprehensive understanding of your competitors. This analysis highlights their motivations and actions and informs your strategic decisions, enabling you to position your business better in the competitive landscape. Use this framework regularly to stay attuned to changes in the competitive environment and adjust your strategies accordingly.

Notes for Your Use

- **Gather Information:** Understand the competitor's motivations, including their strategic goals and driving forces behind their actions.
- **Evaluate:** Analyze management assumptions to identify biases and how they influence strategic decisions. Assess whether these assumptions lead to proactive or reactive strategies.
- **Connect:** Examine the competitor's current strategy versus their intended strategy. Determine effectiveness and predict potential strategic shifts.
- **Develop Strategy:** Evaluate the competitor's capabilities, including their strengths and weaknesses, to anticipate their responses and strategic options.
- **Implement Strategy:** Use insights to inform your strategic decisions, adapt to competitors' potential actions, and maintain a competitive edge.

Competitor Profile Matrix

Brief History

The Competitive Profile Matrix was developed as a strategic management tool to assess and compare the strengths and weaknesses of competing firms. Its origins are rooted in strategic management practices, and it serves as a framework for analyzing key success factors and competitive positions within an industry. The matrix's origins are uncertain as it aggregates many strategic management concepts.

Model 30 of 50: Competitive Profile Matrix

Competitor Profile Matrix

Critical Success Factors	Weight	Our Company		Competitor 1	
		Rating (1–4)	Score	Rating (1–4)	Score
Brand Reputation	0.3	4	1.2	2	0.6
Cost to Supply	0.2	1	0.2	3	0.6
Product Quality	0.2	4	0.8	3	0.6
Product Availability	0.15	3	0.45	3	0.45
Product Price	0.1	4	0.4	2	0.2
Sales Support	0.05	3	0.15	3	0.15
Total	1.00		3.2		2.6

When to Use—Competitive Landscape Comparison

The Competitive Profile Matrix is valuable in strategic decision making when comparing a firm with its rivals. The matrix provides a visual and accurate comparison by highlighting relative strengths and weaknesses using the same factors across a competitor set. The matrix aids in identifying areas for improvement or protection and guiding strategic decisions and actions to enhance the company's competitive position.

Context and Scenario to Use

The Competitive Profile Matrix is utilized across strategic management and competitive analysis in various scenarios and contexts. Here are some scenarios and contexts where the matrix is commonly used:

- **Strategic Planning and Analysis:** Companies use the Competitive Profile Matrix to assess their competitive position relative to key industry competitors. It helps identify strengths and weaknesses, enabling strategic planning to capitalize on strengths and mitigate weaknesses.
- **Market Entry and Expansion:** Companies use the Competitive Profile Matrix to evaluate potential competitors before entering a new market or expanding into a new region.

It provides insights into the competitive landscape, helping to formulate entry strategies and understand competitive threats.

- **Mergers and Acquisitions (M&A):** During M&A activities, the Competitive Profile Matrix assesses target companies' strategic fit and competitive position. It aids in evaluating synergies, identifying complementary strengths, and assessing competitive risks associated with potential acquisitions.

- **Investment and Financial Analysis:** Investors and financial analysts use the Competitive Profile Matrix to evaluate the competitive strength of companies within an industry. It helps assess investment opportunities, predict future performance, and understand competitive dynamics influencing financial outcomes.

- **Competitive Strategy Formulation:** When developing competitive strategies, companies use the Competitive Profile Matrix to prioritize strategic initiatives. It guides decisions on resource allocation, market positioning, and differentiation strategies based on comparative strengths and weaknesses.

- **Industry Analysis and Benchmarking:** Industry analysts and consultants utilize the Competitive Profile Matrix to benchmark companies within an industry. It facilitates industry analysis by identifying industry leaders, assessing competitive pressures, and understanding industry-specific success factors.

- **Strategic Reviews and Performance Monitoring:** Organizations periodically review their competitive position and monitor performance using the Competitive Profile Matrix. This enables ongoing evaluation of competitive strategies, adjustments based on market changes, and continuous improvement in competitive positioning.

The Competitive Profile Matrix is a versatile tool used in strategic management to assess competitive positions, inform strategic decisions, evaluate investment opportunities, and monitor performance in competitive markets across various industries. Its application helps organizations navigate complex, competitive landscapes and effectively achieve strategic objectives.

How to Use

To use a Competitive Profile Matrix, follow these steps:

1. **Identify Critical Success Factors:** Determine vital areas crucial for industry success. These factors, internal (such as cost or efficiency measures) and external (such as product pricing, features, or distribution), should be specific to the industry or strategic group.
2. **Assign Weights:** Assign weights to each critical success factor, ranging from 0.0 (low importance) to 1.0 (high importance), indicating their significance in industry success. The sum of all weights must equal 1.0 to maintain proportionality.
3. **Rate Companies:** Rate each company on the identified critical success factors using a scale from 4 to 1. A rating of 4 signifies a major strength, 3 a minor strength, 2 a minor weakness, and 1 a major weakness.
4. **Utilize Benchmarking:** Compare companies' performance through benchmarking, ensuring equal ratings for similar achievements. For instance, companies with comparable market shares may all receive a rating of 4.
5. **Calculate Scores:** Multiply the weight of each critical success factor by the rating assigned to each. This yields a score for each factor for every company.
6. **Determine Total Scores:** Sum up the individual scores for each company to calculate their total score. The firm with the highest total score is considered relatively more robust in the market.
7. **Analyze Results:** Analyze the Competitive Profile Matrix results to identify each company's competitive strengths and weaknesses. Companies with higher total scores are positioned more competitively.

In summary, the Competitive Profile Matrix provides a structured approach to comparing companies within an industry based on critical success factors. It enables strategic decision making by highlighting competitive advantages and areas needing improvement.

Notes for Your Use

- **Gather Information:** Identify critical success factors crucial for internal and external industry success.
- **Evaluate:** Assign weights to each critical success factor, totaling 1.0, reflecting their importance in the industry.
- **Connect:** Rate each company on these critical success factors from 4 (major strength) to 1 (major weakness). Use benchmarking for consistent ratings.
- **Develop Strategy:** Calculate scores by multiplying the weight of each critical success factor by the company's rating and adding these to get the total scores.
- **Implement Strategy:** Analyze critical success factor scores and total scores to determine competitive strengths and weaknesses, guide strategic decisions, and identify areas for improvement.

Strategic Group Analysis

Brief History

Strategic groups originated from David Hunt's 1972 observation, describing firms within an industry that share similar attributes like cost structure, vertical integration, and product differentiation.[40] Michael Porter (1980) further defined strategic groups as firms pursuing similar strategies, helping organizations identify direct competitors and industry dynamics. Porter also introduced the concept of "mobility barriers," which are obstacles firms must overcome to shift between groups.[41] Short et al. (2007) found that firm-specific factors significantly impact performance, followed by strategic group membership, with industry effects playing a lesser role.[42] Understanding strategic groups and barriers is essential for aligning competitive strategies.

Model 31 of 50: Strategic Group Analysis

Strategic Group Analysis

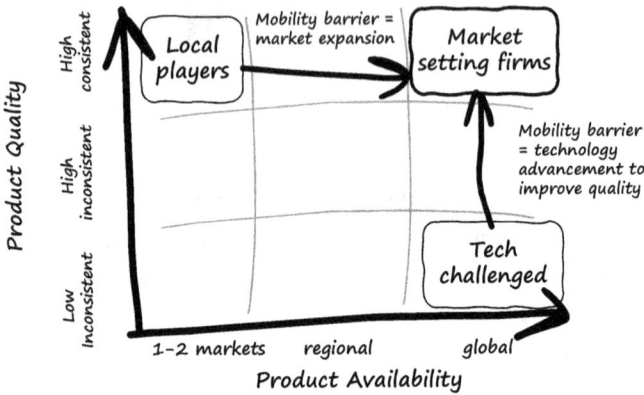

Product Quality (y-axis): High consistent / High inconsistent / Low Inconsistent

Product Availability (x-axis): 1-2 markets / regional / global

Local players

Mobility barrier = market expansion

Market setting firms

Mobility barrier = technology advancement to improve quality

Tech challenged

When to Use—Better Define the True Competitors in the Industry

Strategic group analysis is valuable when seeking a clearer understanding of the firm's "true" competitors within the landscape of broad industry competition. By identifying firms with similar competitive attributes through a strategic group map, you can unveil important distinctions among competitive positions and barriers to mobility across groups. This analysis aids in explaining subtle performance differences within a tightly grouped set of competitors with similar characteristics, such as size, pricing, features, target market, and distribution channels. Strategic group analysis enhances visibility into competitive dynamics, narrows the competitive set, and guides strategic decision making. The analysis also aids in understanding the barriers to moving between groups. Strategic group analysis links very well with the Competitive Profile Matrix. The critical success factors of the Competitive Profile Matrix may be similar to the characteristics of strategic grouping.

Context and Scenario to Use

Strategic Group Analysis is a valuable tools in various scenarios and contexts within strategic management. Here are some specific applications:

- **Industry Analysis:** A consulting firm conducts an industry analysis for a client looking to understand competitive dynamics in the automotive industry. The firm uses Strategic Group Analysis to identify clusters of competitors based on factors like product range, pricing strategies, and technological innovation. This helps the client understand where their competitors are positioned and identify potential areas for differentiation.

- **Competitive Benchmarking:** A company wants to benchmark its performance against key competitors in the retail sector. By mapping strategic groups, the company can compare its strategies and performance metrics (such as price, quality, and customer service) against those of direct competitors within the same strategic group. This aids in identifying strengths and weaknesses.

- **Market Entry Strategy:** A tech start-up plans to enter the smartphone market and needs to identify the most favorable segment to target. Strategic Group Mapping helps the start-up visualize the competitive landscape, identify groups with less competition, and tailor its entry strategy to exploit gaps or underserved segments in the market.

- **Merger and Acquisition (M&A) Evaluation:** A company considering an acquisition needs to evaluate the target company's strategic fit within its industry. Using Strategic Group Analysis, the company can assess how the target company's strategic position aligns with its own and whether the acquisition would enhance its competitive advantage or create strategic synergies.

- **Strategic Planning and Resource Allocation:** A multinational corporation reviews its strategic plan and decides to allocate resources across different business units. By mapping strategic groups within each industry segment, the corporation can identify which units are in highly competitive groups. These units may need more investment than those in less competitive groups where growth opportunities are higher.

- **Identifying Market Opportunities and Threats:** An FMCG company wants to innovate and launch new products but needs to understand potential threats from competitors. Strategic Group Analysis can reveal which groups of competitors are most likely to respond aggressively to new entrants or innovations, helping the company anticipate and plan for competitive reactions.

- **Assessing Strategic Changes:** A pharmaceutical company is considering shifting its strategic focus from generic drugs to high-end specialty drugs. The company uses Strategic Group Mapping to understand the competitive landscape in the specialty drugs market, identify key players, and evaluate the barriers to entry and potential competitive pressures in this new strategic group.

Strategic Group Analysis is a versatile tools that provide insights into competitive dynamics, helping businesses make informed strategic decisions. Whether it's for market entry, competitive benchmarking, M&A evaluation, or strategic planning, these tools help identify competitive positions and guide strategic initiatives in complex and dynamic industries.

How to Use

Using Strategic Group Analysis involves a systematic process to analyze and visualize the competitive landscape within an industry. Here's a step-by-step guide:

1. **Identify Differentiating Characteristics:** Identify key characteristics that differentiate companies within the industry. This could include product offerings, pricing strategies, distribution channels, technological aspects, or customer services. Consider the most critical differentiation characteristics from an external customer's and internal corporate perspectives. These are the x- and y-axis on the matrix.
2. **Plot Companies on the Map:** Plot each company on the strategic group map based on the identified differentiating characteristics. Then, group them based on similarities, forming strategic groups.

3. **Draw Circles Proportional to Sales Share:** Draw circles around each strategic group and make their size proportional to the respective group's share of total industry sales. This will visually represent each strategic group's market presence and importance.

4. **Identify Competitors and Cross-Group Rivals:** Identify direct competitors by looking at companies within the same circle (strategic group). Also, consider cross-group rivals by examining closer circles on the map. Proximity may indicate potential competition or areas of overlap.

5. **Analyze Gaps on the Map:** Examine the gaps between strategic groups on the map. These gaps reveal untapped market potential and potential business opportunities. Understanding these gaps can guide strategic decisions, helping identify areas where a company could differentiate itself or explore new market segments.

Additional considerations:

- **Dynamic Nature of Strategic Groups:** Recognize that strategic groups can shift over time due to changing customer needs, evolving technologies, or market shifts. Avoid assuming that a firm is permanently locked into a specific strategic group.
- **Emergence and Disappearance of Strategic Groups:** Understand that entire strategic groups and their constituent firms can emerge or disappear over time. Changes in competitive conditions may lead to their decline or evolution.
- **Understand the Mobility Barriers:** Identify the barriers that prevent competitors from moving across groups and the strength of the group barriers.
- **Consolidation Trends:** Acknowledge the trend of consolidation within industries. Mergers and acquisitions among competitors can reshape the competitive landscape, influencing the stability and membership of strategic groups.

A strategic group map visually represents competitive dynamics, helping businesses identify opportunities, competitors, and areas for strategic focus within their industry.

Notes for Your Use

- **Gather Information:** Identify key differentiating characteristics within your industry such as product offerings, pricing strategies, and distribution channels.
- **Evaluate:** Plot companies based on these characteristics on the map, grouping them into strategic clusters.
- **Connect:** Draw circles around each group, with sizes proportional to their market share, to visualize market presence and importance.
- **Develop Strategy:** Identify direct competitors within the same group and cross-group rivals in close proximity. Analyze gaps between groups to spot market opportunities or barriers to mobility.
- **Implement Strategy:** Use insights to explore new market segments, address gaps, and adapt strategies to shifting competitive dynamics.

Red Queen Effect

Brief History

Inspired by Lewis Carroll's *Through the Looking-Glass*, the Red Queen effect describes how businesses must constantly innovate to maintain their position, much like the Red Queen's paradoxical race where running fast only keeps you in the same spot. This concept, originating from evolutionary theory by Leigh Van Valen, illustrates the challenge of gaining a lasting advantage in a competitive environment.[43] In 2005, Voelpel et al. addressed this phenomenon in their article "Escaping the Red Queen Effect in Competitive Strategy," published in the *European Management Journal*.[44] They proposed that firms break free from this cycle by rethinking business models and challenging industry norms, thereby securing sustainable advantages.

Model 32 of 50: Red Queen Effect

Red Queen Effect

	Assess Your Competitors	Assess Yourself	Similarities	Differences
Value Proposition				
Technologies (innovations)				
Capital Resources				
Customer Segments				
Collaborators				
Etc.				

When to Use—Assess the Similarities Across the Competitive Landscape

The Red Queen effect in strategy emphasizes the need for agility, foresight, and proactive management to achieve long-term success in a competitive environment where others are also advancing. It warns that simply repeating past successes without adapting can lead to decline as competition continuously evolves. This concept urges companies to evaluate the similarities and differences in evolution. By applying the Red Queen effect, you can challenge your team to broaden their perspective of the competitive landscape and encourage them to rethink strategies in a way that diverts from similarities and increases competitive intensity.

Context and Scenario to Use

The Red Queen effect helps you view the competitive landscape more broadly, encouraging a shift from "working harder" to "working differently" to gain a competitive advantage. While working differently poses near-term risks, it offers long-term benefits. Red Queen thinking (working harder to outpace competition) is most detrimental under conditions such as new competitive entry, slowing rates of improvement or differentiation, and intense head-to-head competition. Here are specific examples:

- **Market Positioning:** Companies strive to innovate and improve their offerings to maintain or enhance their market position. For instance, companies like Apple and Samsung continuously release new models with advanced features in the smartphone industry. Despite these efforts, competitors quickly catch up, leading to a continuous innovation cycle with diminishing returns on differentiation. This results in high costs and marginal gains in market share.

- **Product Development:** In the tech industry, firms like Microsoft and Google invest heavily in product development to stay ahead. Similar advancements quickly follow Microsoft's updates to its Windows operating system in Google's Chrome OS. This constant leapfrogging in features and functionalities demonstrates the Red Queen effect, where each company's efforts to outpace the other lead to rapid yet necessary advancements, often with limited long-term competitive advantage.

- **Cybersecurity:** The cybersecurity field exemplifies the Red Queen effect. As companies develop new security measures to protect against cyber threats, hackers simultaneously establish new methods to breach those defenses. This necessitates a continuous cycle of updates and innovations in security protocols. Organizations must invest heavily in staying ahead of potential threats, but the ever-evolving nature of cyberattacks means they are often only temporarily secure.

- **Consumer Goods:** In the fast-moving consumer goods sector, Coca-Cola and Pepsi compete constantly. Both companies regularly launch new products and marketing campaigns to capture consumer interest. However, each new initiative is quickly countered by the other, leading to a dynamic but stable competitive environment. This constant rivalry exemplifies the Red Queen effect, where both companies must continually innovate to maintain their market positions.

In all these scenarios, the Red Queen effect emphasizes the necessity of continuous improvement and adaptation to maintain relative advantage or even to keep up with competitors. Organizations that recognize this can shift their strategies to "working differently," fostering long-term growth and resilience.

How to Use

For companies engaged in a Red Queen effect, sustainable competitive advantage is moving beyond focusing on the current competition to understanding the broader, systemic business landscape. By doing so, they can reinvent their business models and strategically innovate for long-term success. To use the Red Queen effect in business strategy, consider the following steps:

1. **Evaluate the Competitive Landscape:** Identify your competitors and assess their evolution. Look at their innovations, market strategies, and improvements to understand the pace of industry change.

2. **Analyze Your Own Progress:** Examine your company's performance and strategy over time. Are you advancing, or are you maintaining the same position despite efforts? This will help recognize if you are caught in the Red Queen effect, where constant improvement yields no relative competitive gain.

3. **Foster a Culture of Innovation:** Encourage your team to think beyond incremental improvements. Aim for transformative innovation by developing new business models or rethinking customer needs and market positioning.

4. **Disrupt Industry Norms:** Consider how you can redefine industry standards or challenge existing norms. This could involve leveraging technology, changing your value proposition, or adopting new operational processes.

5. **Experiment and Sense-Test:** As Voelpel et al. (2005) suggested, sense-testing new ideas and strategies can help identify opportunities to break free from the competition's pace. Experiment with business models to see what can provide lasting competitive advantages.

6. **Adapt and Evolve Continuously:** The Red Queen effect underscores the importance of staying agile. Even after gaining an edge, remain proactive by continually adapting to market changes and competitor moves.

By applying these steps, you can avoid stagnation and ensure sustained progress in a fast-evolving competitive landscape.

Notes for Your Use

- **Gather Information:** Continuously analyze customer insights to identify emerging trends and evolving needs. Monitor behavioral shifts and explore new value propositions to enhance engagement and stay ahead of competitors.
- **Evaluate:** Stay up-to-date with technological advancements and assess their potential to redefine customer value propositions and improve operational efficiencies. Understand how these changes might impact your competitive position.
- **Connect:** Observe changes in business infrastructure, including supplier and buyer networks. Identify new market entrants and evolving network dynamics to anticipate competitive pressures.
- **Develop Strategy:** Analyze how economic and industry shifts affect profitability and the competitive landscape. Develop strategies that allow you to adapt your business model proactively rather than reactively.
- **Implement Strategy:** Use gathered insights to innovate and evolve your business model. Aim to continuously adapt and enhance your offerings to maintain a competitive edge and avoid the pitfalls of a Red Queen race, where you're constantly running to stay in place.

Co-opetition

Brief History

In 1996, Adam M. Brandenburger and Barry J. Nalebuff introduced the concept of co-opetition in their book *Co-Opetition*.[45] Drawing on game theory, they proposed co-opetition as a strategy for businesses to actively shape the competitive landscape by considering both cooperative and competitive dynamics. By viewing the competitive environment as a system, co-opetition encourages companies to identify win-win and win-lose opportunities with various stakeholders, including competitors, to craft more effective business strategies.

Model 33 of 50: Co-opetition Matrix

Co-opetition

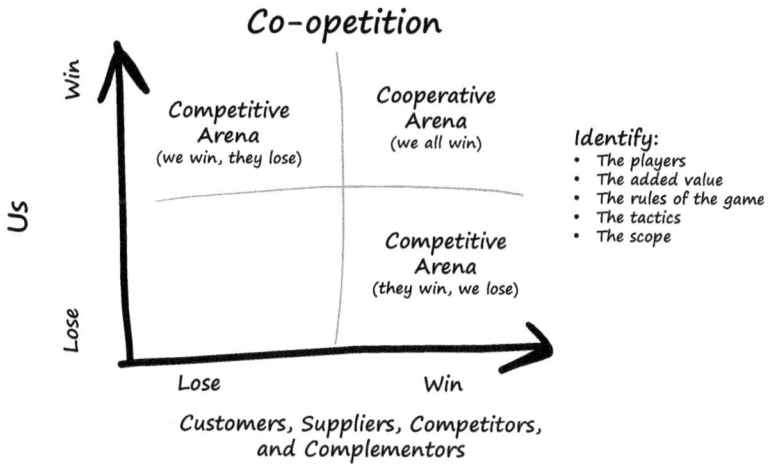

Customers, Suppliers, Competitors,
and Complementors

When to Use—Assessing the Competitive Landscape for Competitive Partnering

Co-opetition is valuable when a strategic perspective is needed to move beyond the traditional win-lose competition model. It involves four key players: customers, suppliers, competitors, and complementors. The approach encourages strategic thinking about business relationships through five basic elements: players, added value, rules, tactics, and scope. The goal is to view business as a blend of warfare and peace, cooperating with some players to create or expand the market ("the pie") while competing with others to capture a market share. Businesses should clearly understand when and where they are participating in competitive or cooperative arenas. This strategic blend helps businesses innovate, grow, and thrive in complex, competitive environments.

Context and Scenario to Use

Co-opetition is versatile and applicable across various contexts. It allows you to blend cooperation and competition strategically to achieve mutual benefits, drive innovation, and enhance their competitive positioning in dynamic market environments. Here are some examples:

- **Industry Alliances and Partnerships:** In industries where technological advancements or regulatory changes require significant investment, co-opetition can help companies share resources and expertise. For example, automotive manufacturers might collaborate to develop new electric vehicle technologies while competing for customers.

- **Market Expansion and New Entrants:** When entering new markets, companies can use co-opetition to collaborate with local firms to gain market insights and share distribution channels. For instance, a multinational company entering an emerging market might partner with local businesses to understand consumer behavior and navigate regulatory landscapes.

- **Innovation and Research:** Cooperation is beneficial in sectors that demand continuous innovation, such as pharmaceuticals or technology. Companies can collaborate on R&D projects to share innovation's high costs and risks. For example, pharmaceutical companies might collaborate on drug research while competing to market the final products.

- **Standard Setting:** In industries where establishing common standards is crucial, such as telecommunications or software, companies can cooperate to develop standards that benefit the entire industry. This collaboration helps ensure compatibility and drives industry-wide growth while companies compete on other fronts.

- **Supply Chain Optimization:** Companies can collaborate with suppliers and competitors to optimize supply chains, reduce costs, and improve efficiencies. For instance, retail competitors might share logistics networks to minimize transportation costs and improve delivery times.

- **Enhancing Customer Value:** Businesses can partner to offer bundled services or products that provide greater customer value. For example, airlines and hotel chains often collaborate to offer travel packages that enhance the customer experience while still competing for individual customer loyalty.

- **Crisis Management and Sustainability Initiatives:** During crises like natural disasters or global pandemics, companies might collaborate to address shared challenges. Additionally, co-opetition can support sustainability initiatives where companies work together to achieve environmental goals while maintaining competitive differentiation.
- **Competitive Differentiation:** In highly competitive markets, companies can use co-opetition to differentiate themselves. For example, two competing firms might collaborate on a public awareness campaign about industry benefits while continuing to compete on product features and pricing.

How to Use

Co-opetition is implemented through game theory or by developing hypothetical testing strategies. Central to the concept is "added value," which describes the value each player (customers, suppliers, competitors, and complementors) brings to the competitive landscape. Brandenburger and Nalebuff's PARTS framework helps determine the competitive system:

1. **Players**
   Definition: Any change in players alters the game.
   Assessment: Identify how changes in the players affect the dynamics of the game. For instance:
   - Customers: Determine how customer preferences and behaviors shift with the introduction of new players.
   - Suppliers: Evaluate how changes in suppliers impact supply chain efficiency and costs.
   - Competitors: Analyze how new competitors entering the market affect competitive pressures and market share distribution.
   - Complementors: Assess how new complementors can enhance the value of your offerings and create synergies.

2. **Added Value**

   Definition: The impact of each player on the total value of the game.

   Assessment: Evaluate how the entry or exit of players influences the overall value:

   - Power Dynamics: Examine how changes affect the relative power of players. For example, does the introduction of a new competitor shift bargaining power to customers?
   - Market Demand: Consider how increased demand in a new market can elevate the value of existing players by driving up prices due to limited supply.
   - Value Creation: Identify opportunities to create additional value through collaboration with complementors.

3. **Rules**

   Definition: The guidelines governing the game.

   Assessment: Adjust rules to favor your position:

   - Cost Advantages: Utilize cost advantages to implement favorable contractual terms, such as "meet-the-competition" clauses, to maintain market position.
   - Regulatory Changes: Adapt to or influence regulatory changes that can enhance your competitive edge.
   - Industry Standards: Set or influence industry standards that align with your strengths.

4. **Tactics**

   Definition: The strategies to influence other players.

   Assessment: Determine when to be transparent and when to remain opaque:

   - Market Positioning: Clearly communicate strengths, such as new technologies or superior product features, to establish market leadership.
   - Competitive Moves: Anticipate and react to competitors' strategies by selectively revealing your tactics to influence their actions.
   - Negotiation Strategies: Use transparency to build trust with key partners while maintaining strategic ambiguity with competitors.

5. **Scope**

Definition: The boundaries and interconnectedness of the game.

Assessment: Understand the broader implications of strategic moves:

- Future Moves: Analyze how current actions affect future opportunities and threats.
- Player Dynamics: Recognize that competitors can become complementors and vice versa, affecting long-term strategic alliances.
- Market Expansion: Consider how expanding into new markets or segments can impact the overall competitive landscape and create new opportunities for cooperation.

By systematically addressing the PARTS framework, the competitive landscape can be better understood. This enables you to craft optimal strategies that transform win-lose scenarios into win-win outcomes.

Notes for Your Use

- **Gather Information:** Identify key players (customers, suppliers, competitors, complementors) and their roles in the competitive landscape.
- **Evaluate:** Assess each player's added value, including how their entry or exit influences overall market dynamics and power structures.
- **Connect:** Adjust rules to optimize your position, leveraging cost advantages, regulatory changes, and industry standards.
- **Develop Strategy:** Formulate tactics based on transparency and strategic ambiguity to position your strengths and influence competitors.
- **Implement Strategy:** Understand the scope of strategic moves, considering future implications, player dynamics, and market expansion opportunities.

Competitor Checklist

The final model serves as a structured guide, organizing the discussion and linking to models in Section 4. As you go through the checklist, dive deep into understanding the competitive intensity of your market, your competitors' future moves, your strengths and weaknesses, the organization of the competitive landscape, and potential actions to disrupt the current competitive structure.

Start by analyzing your industry's competitive concentration, particularly the positions of major players. Understand where your business fits within the broader competitive landscape and identify barriers that support your position or pose challenges.

Next, assess your key competitors' internal ambitions and external capabilities. Consider their potential future actions and how they might impact your strategy. Analyze the critical success factors in your industry to determine where you hold an advantage or disadvantage.

Narrow your focus by grouping similar competitors and analyzing how these groups differentiate themselves. Identify the mobility barriers between groups and evaluate their strength. Determine if your strategy aligns with or requires overcoming these barriers.

Finally, assess the pace of change in your industry compared to your activities. Are competitors moving forward while you remain stagnant? Are you keeping pace, or is there an opportunity to break the competitive structure? Consider whether co-opetition—collaborating with a competitor—could create new opportunities and expand the market.

By following this checklist and thoroughly analyzing your competitive environment, you can develop strategies that navigate or disrupt the competitive landscape, allowing your business to grow beyond traditional competition.

Model 34 of 50: Competitor Checklist

Question	Tools	Your team's thoughts
How competitively intense is our industry?	HHI Rule of 3 & 4	
What drives our competitors' actions?	Porter's 4 Corners	
How do we perform versus our competitors?	Competitor Profile Matrix	
What are the competitive groupings and barriers?	Strategic Group Analysis	
Are we staying ahead in the race?	Red Queen Effect	
Can we change the structure with cooperation	Co-opetition	

SECTION 5

Climate: Inferential and Uncontrollable

Assess your strategy within the changing climate that your organization operates.

Venturing into the Climate band entails a deeper reduction in control and information. Models within this band provide valuable insights into the expansive environment surrounding your company. The Climate band evaluates governmental advantages, policies, and economic factors, broadening its scope to encompass the entire value chain—raw materials, manufacturing, channels, and selling entities. Every facet constituting the company's operational landscape is encapsulated within the Climate.

This section focuses on identifying critical externalities—factors outside your organization's control—that could significantly impact your operations. Understanding both predictable and uncertain changes in the external environment is essential. You can integrate those that are predictable into your strategy. However, for uncertain factors, it's crucial to monitor their development closely and build flexibility into your strategy to address potential shifts over the time horizon. A thorough understanding of these external factors enables your organization to adapt and build resilience, ensuring your strategy remains effective despite unforeseen changes in the broader climate.

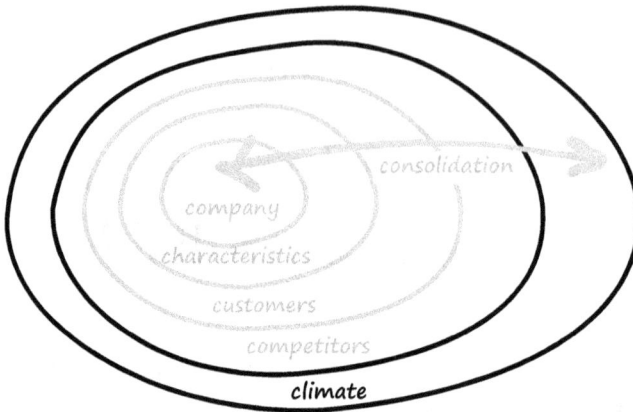

Quick exercise with your team:

Start your climate assessment the same way you did in all prior sections. Conduct leadership interviews or a leadership workshop, and ask a few simple questions to understand your organization's starting point.

Questions:
- *How could the broad environment landscape change?*
- *What country/regional advantages exist? Can they change?*
- *How could industry dynamics change?*
- *How could industry value move?*
- *How has the industry evolved?*
- *How can the industry change in the future?*

CAGE Analysis

Brief History

In his 2001 article "Distance Still Matters: The Hard Reality of Global Expansion," Pankaj Ghemawat argues that geographic distance remains a significant barrier to global expansion despite the growing interconnectedness of markets.[46] He introduces the CAGE framework— Cultural, Administrative, Geographic, and Economic distances—to explain the challenges companies face when entering foreign markets. Ghemawat emphasizes that these differences affect cross-border business more than commonly believed and warns against assuming that globalization has minimized the impact of distance.

Model 35 of 50: CAGE Model

CAGE Model

Cultural	Administration	Geographic	Economic
Language	Political Systems / Stability	Physical Distance / Time Zones	Income Levels
Norms / Values			Economic Development
Religion	Regulations and Legal Frameworks	Transportation Infrastructure	Cost Structures
Business Etiquette	Trade Agreements		Natural Resources
Etc.	Government Policies	Climate / Geography	Input Availability
	Etc.	Etc.	Etc.

When to Use—Evaluating Your Host and Home Country Distances

Corporations use the CAGE model to analyze the impact of cultural, administrative, geographic, and economic distances on international business operations. The model helps them make informed decisions about market entry, strategic planning, risk assessment, and partner selection. By understanding these distances, companies can tailor their strategies to better fit local markets, optimize supply chains, and enhance their competitive advantage. The model provides a structured approach to identifying potential barriers and opportunities in foreign markets, ensuring more effective and efficient international expansion and operations.

Context and Scenarios of Use

The CAGE model is used in international business to analyze and understand the impact of distance on cross-border operations and market entry strategies. Here are some scenarios when the CAGE model is beneficial:

- **Market Entry Decisions:** When a company is considering entering a new international market, the CAGE model helps assess the potential challenges and opportunities based on the cultural, administrative, geographic, and economic distances between the home country and the target market.

- **Strategic Planning:** For developing long-term strategies, the CAGE model assists in identifying which international markets are more attractive and feasible for expansion, considering the distances that might affect business operations.
- **Risk Assessment:** The CAGE model helps evaluate the risks associated with entering or operating in a foreign market by highlighting the differences that could lead to misunderstandings, operational inefficiencies, or regulatory challenges.
- **Partner Selection:** When selecting partners for joint ventures, alliances, or supply chain collaborations, the CAGE model helps understand potential friction points and synergies based on distances.
- **Competitive Analysis:** To analyze competitors' performance in different markets, the CAGE model can show how distance factors might influence their success or challenges.
- **Customization of Marketing Strategies:** The model helps tailor marketing strategies to different international markets by understanding the cultural and economic differences that influence consumer behavior.
- **Policy Formulation:** Governments and policy makers use the CAGE model to understand the barriers to international trade and investment and to design policies that mitigate these barriers.

By systematically evaluating the four dimensions of distance (cultural, administrative, geographic, and economic), you can make more informed decisions about international operations and strategies.

How to Use

To use the CAGE model, assess each current (or home) market against the target market. Below are some steps to begin the evaluation:

1. **Cultural Distance:**
   - **Language:** Identify and understand the primary languages spoken in the target market. Consider the need for translation

and localization of products, marketing materials, and customer support.

- ○ **Values and Norms**: Research the societal values, customs, and norms that influence consumer behavior and business practices. Understand cultural differences in communication styles, decision-making processes, and negotiation tactics.
- ○ **Religion**: Analyze the dominant religions in the target market and their impact on consumer preferences, holidays, and work practices.
- ○ **Business Etiquette**: Study the social norms and business etiquette to ensure respectful and effective interactions with local stakeholders.

2. **Administrative Distance:**
   - ○ **Political Systems**: Examine the type of government, political stability, and the presence of any political risks that might affect business operations.
   - ○ **Regulations and Legal Frameworks**: Investigate the legal environment, including regulations related to trade, labor, intellectual property, taxation, and corporate governance.
   - ○ **Trade Agreements**: Identify any existing trade agreements, tariffs, and trade barriers between the home country and the target market.
   - ○ **Government Policies**: Analyze government policies and incentives that may support or hinder business activities, such as subsidies, import/export restrictions, and foreign investment regulations.

3. **Geographic Distance:**
   - ○ **Physical Distance**: Measure the physical distance between the home country and the target market. Consider the impact on transportation costs, delivery times, and logistics.
   - ○ **Transportation Infrastructure**: Assess the quality and availability of transportation infrastructure, including roads, ports, airports, and railways. Evaluate the ease of moving goods and people within the target market.
   - ○ **Time Zones**: Understand the time zone differences and their implications for communication, coordination, and real-time operations.

- ○ **Climate and Geography**: Consider the geographic and climatic conditions that may affect product demand, supply chain operations, and overall business activities.

4. **Economic Distance:**
   - ○ **Income Levels**: Compare the income levels and purchasing power of consumers in the target market. Understand the economic disparities that may influence pricing and product positioning.
   - ○ **Economic Development**: Evaluate the level of economic development, including infrastructure, industrialization, and technological advancement. Assess the market's capacity to support your products or services.
   - ○ **Cost Structures**: Analyze the cost structures related to labor, materials, production, and distribution in the target market. Compare these costs to those in the home country to identify potential advantages or challenges.
   - ○ **Natural Resources and Inputs**: Identify the availability and quality of natural resources, raw materials, and other inputs required for your business operations in the target market.

By thoroughly gathering information in these areas, you can comprehensively understand the target market's characteristics and potential barriers to entry. This analysis forms the foundation for developing effective international strategies and making informed business decisions.

Notes for Your Use

- **Gather Information:** Collect data on cultural, administrative, geographic, and economic differences between the home market and the target market.
- **Evaluate:** Assess the impact of these differences on business operations, identifying potential challenges and opportunities.
- **Connect:** Identify how these factors influence your business model and where adjustments are needed.

- **Develop Strategy:** Formulate strategies to address challenges, adapting marketing, operations, and logistics to fit the target market.
- **Implement Strategy:** Execute the strategies, monitor performance, and continuously optimize based on feedback and changing market conditions.

PESTEL

Brief History

In his 1967 book *Scanning the Business Environment*, Harvard professor Francis Aguilar introduced the ETPS framework for Economic, Technical, Political, and Social factors.[47] This framework was designed to help businesses systematically analyze external environmental factors that could impact their operations. Companies can better anticipate environmental changes and make strategic decisions by examining these four key areas. ETPS later evolved into the widely known PEST (Political, Economic, Social, and Technological) and PESTEL (adding Environmental and Legal) analysis. However, Aguilar's original framework laid the foundation for understanding how external forces shape business strategies.

Model 36 of 50: PESTEL

PESTEL

Political	Economic	Social	Technological	Environmental	Legal
Government Policy (trade, tax, labor) Political Stability (corruption) Trade Agreements Etc.	Economic Growth Interest Rates Inflation Rates Exchange Rates Etc.	Population Growth Age Cultural Differences Consumer Behavior Etc.	Innovation levels Technological Advancement Rates R&D activities Disruptive Technology Etc.	Climate / Environmental Policies Sustainability trends Etc.	Patent / Copyright laws Employment laws Consumer protection laws Etc.

When to Use—Evaluating Your External Business Environment

PESTEL analysis is essential in strategy when evaluating macroeconomic factors impacting an organization. PESTEL analysis aids in identifying potential threats, weaknesses, and opportunities within the marketing environment. This framework provides a comprehensive understanding, enabling effective strategic decision making and adaptation to external influences.

Context and Scenarios of Use

PESTEL analyzes macro-environmental factors—Political, Economic, Social, Technological, Environmental, and Legal—to guide strategic planning and risk management. Here are some scenarios where the PESTEL is useful.

- **Strategic Planning:** PESTEL analysis helps businesses understand the macro-environmental factors influencing their operations, aiding in long-term strategic planning and decision making.
- **Market Entry:** When entering a new market, PESTEL analysis evaluates the external environment to identify potential risks and opportunities, ensuring informed market entry strategies.
- **Risk Management:** By assessing political, economic, social, technological, environmental, and legal factors, PESTEL analysis helps identify and mitigate potential risks that could impact business operations.
- **Product Development:** Understanding external factors through PESTEL can guide product development strategies, ensuring products meet market demands and comply with regulatory requirements.
- **Competitor Analysis:** PESTEL analysis provides insights into the external factors affecting competitors, helping businesses understand their competitive landscape and identify areas for differentiation.

- **Investment Decisions:** Investors use PESTEL analysis to evaluate the macro-environmental conditions that could impact the profitability and sustainability of potential investments.

By systematically analyzing these external factors, businesses can better navigate the complexities of their operating environment and make more informed strategic decisions.

How to Use

To conduct a comprehensive PESTEL analysis, systematically assess each component to gain insights into the external factors influencing an organization and how those factors have changed and possibly could change over time:

1. **Political Factors:** Identify government policies, regulations, and stability affecting business operations. Analyze trade agreements and assess potential political risks.
2. **Economic Factors:** Evaluate economic indicators, inflation rates, interest rates, and currency exchange rates. Assess market conditions and analyze economic trends influencing the entity.
3. **Sociocultural Factors:** Identify societal and demographic influences on consumer behavior. Analyze cultural trends, social attitudes, and lifestyle changes affecting the entity. Consider potential societal changes and their impact.
4. **Technological Factors:** Identify technological innovations, trends, and disruptions relevant to operations. Analyze the rate of technological change and its potential effects on the entity.
5. **Environmental Factors:** Identify environmental regulations, climate change impacts, and sustainability trends. Analyze ecological factors and assess compliance with environmental standards.
6. **Legal Factors:** Identify laws, regulations, and legal issues affecting business operations. Analyze industry standards, contractual obligations, and potential legal risks. Consider legal compliance and the implications for the organization.

Throughout the analysis, consider the interconnectedness of these factors and their collective impact on the organization's strategic decisions. Assessing potential risks and opportunities in each category enables a more holistic understanding of the external environment. After evaluating each category, consider consolidation across categories and summarize the most critical factors and the potential impact of those most critical factors on the organization. This insight into the most critical factors and implications of those factors on the organization guides strategic planning, helping the organization adapt and thrive in a dynamic and ever-changing business landscape.

Notes for Your Use

- **Gather Data:** Collect information on political, economic, sociocultural, technological, environmental, and legal factors affecting the organization.
- **Evaluate Impact:** Analyze how these external factors influence business operations, identifying risks and opportunities.
- **Assess Interconnectedness:** Examine how these factors interact and shape overall strategic decisions.
- **Develop Strategies:** Use insights to create strategies that address external risks and capitalize on opportunities.
- **Monitor and Adapt:** Continuously track external changes and adjust strategies to stay resilient and agile in a dynamic environment.

Porter's Diamond of National Advantage

Brief History

Michael Porter introduced the Diamond Model in his 1990 book, *The Competitive Advantage of Nations.*[48] This diamond-shaped framework explores the factors influencing the international competitiveness of a nation's industries. The model focuses on firm strategy, structure/rivalry, factor conditions, demand conditions, and related and supporting industries. Porter's Diamond Model has since become a key concept in understanding the competitive advantage of nations and shaping strategies for economic development.

Model 37 of 50: *Porter's Diamond of National Advantage*

Porter's Diamond

Factor Conditions	Demand Conditions	Related & Supporting Industries	Firm Strategy, Structure & Rivalry
Labor Natural Resources Capital Infrastructure Technology Etc.	Domestic Markets Customer Preference Market Sophistication Etc.	Supporting Industries Suppliers Supply Chain Market Channels Etc.	Competitiveness Management Strength Firm Advantages Etc.

When to Use—*Competitiveness of Industries in a Specific Country or Region*

Use Porter's Diamond Model when analyzing the competitiveness of industries in specific countries or regions. This model is valuable for understanding why certain areas have a competitive advantage, considering factors like factor conditions, domestic demand, supporting industries, and the overall business environment. Porter's Diamond Model helps identify strategies to enhance competitiveness by addressing various elements simultaneously, acknowledging the interconnected nature of these factors in shaping the success of industries on a global scale.

Context and Scenarios of Use

Michael Porter's Diamond Model is used to analyze and understand the competitive advantage of nations or regions. Here are some scenarios where the Diamond Model can be applied:

- **National Economic Policy Formulation:** Governments can use the model to identify areas where their country's industries are competitive or lacking. By understanding the factors influencing competitive advantage, policy makers can craft strategies to enhance national competitiveness, such as investing in education, improving infrastructure, or fostering innovation.

- **Industry Analysis:** Companies looking to enter or expand in a foreign market can use the model to evaluate the country's competitive environment. This helps them understand local factors like demand conditions and related industries, which can impact their strategy and potential success.
- **Regional Development Strategies:** Regional governments and development agencies can apply the model to identify strengths and weaknesses in their region's competitive position. This analysis can guide initiatives to boost regional industries, attract investment, and improve local infrastructure.
- **Comparative Advantage Analysis:** Businesses and investors can use the model to compare the competitive advantages of different countries or regions. This helps make informed decisions about where to invest, which markets to enter, or which suppliers to partner with.
- **Benchmarking and Best Practices:** Firms can use the model to benchmark their performance against competitors in other countries. By analyzing factors like firm strategy and related industries, companies can identify best practices and areas for improvement.
- **Strategic Planning:** Companies looking to develop international strategies can use the Diamond Model to assess how well they align with the competitive factors of different markets. This helps in refining strategic approaches to leverage national advantages and mitigate disadvantages.
- **Innovation and R&D Focus:** Understanding the local demand conditions and related industries can guide firms in focusing their R&D efforts. For example, a company might focus on innovations that cater specifically to the needs of the domestic market or build upon the strengths of related industries.

The Diamond Model provides a structured way to analyze how various factors interact and influence competitive advantage in each scenario, helping you make more informed strategic decisions.

How to Use

To use Porter's Diamond Model in developing a business strategy, start by analyzing the four key elements:

1. **Factor Conditions:** Assess the nation's or region's endowments regarding labor, natural resources, capital, infrastructure, and technological capabilities. Identify strengths and weaknesses in these factors and understand how they contribute to or hinder industry competitiveness.
2. **Demand Conditions:** Examine the nature and size of the domestic market. Understand customer preferences, needs, and the level of market sophistication. Analyze the factors that shape local demand and how they influence industry competitiveness.
3. **Related and Supporting Industries:** Evaluate the presence and strength of supporting industries, suppliers, and the supply chain. Identify areas where improvements or collaborations can enhance the competitiveness of the entire industry. Consider the interdependence between different sectors.
4. **Firm Strategy, Structure, and Rivalry:** Analyze the nation's or region's competitive dynamics. Assess the level of competition, management practices, and the overall business environment. Understand how firms strategize, structure their operations, and compete with each other.

Recognize the interconnectedness of these elements and how changes in one area can affect the others. For example, upgrading technological capabilities (Factor Conditions) can impact product innovation and quality, influencing demand conditions. Enhancing collaboration within the supply chain (Related and Supporting Industries) can improve overall industry efficiency.

To develop a robust business strategy, leverage insights from each element to identify areas for improvement or investment. For instance, if demand conditions reveal a sophisticated local market, consider strategies for catering to these preferences. Collaborate with related industries to strengthen the entire value chain.

Notes for Your Use

- **Gather Information:** Assess factor conditions such as labor, resources, infrastructure, and technological capabilities. Collect data on local demand, supporting industries, and competitive dynamics.
- **Evaluate:** Analyze how these factors impact industry competitiveness. Understand customer preferences (demand conditions), assess the strength of suppliers, and review firm strategies and market rivalry.
- **Connect:** Examine how these elements interact. For example, technological advancements (factor conditions) may influence product innovation and demand. Collaboration with supporting industries can enhance efficiency.
- **Develop Strategy:** Leverage insights to identify areas for improvement. Tailor strategies to address sophisticated local demand, improve supply chain efficiency, and strengthen competitive positioning.
- **Implement Strategy:** Apply these strategies by investing in key areas, fostering industry collaborations, and continuously adapting to evolving competitive conditions.

Porter's Five Forces

Brief History

Porter's Five Forces framework, introduced in his 1980 book *Competitive Strategy: Techniques for Analyzing Industries and Competitors*, originated as a tool to assess industry competitive dynamics.[49] Porter identified five fundamental forces—threat of new entrants, bargaining power of suppliers, bargaining power of buyers, threat of substitutes, and intensity of rivalry—that shape the profitability and competition in any market. The model emphasizes how these forces influence strategic decisions and guide businesses to improve their competitive position.

Model 38 of 50: Porter's Five Forces

Porter's 5 Forces

Competitive Rivalry	Threat of New Entrants	Threat of Substitutes	Supplier Power	Buyer Power
Competitive Concentration	Barriers of Entry	Availability of Alternative	Supplier Concentration	Buyer Concentration
Market Growth	Capital Requirements	Switching Costs	Supplier Dependency	Buyer Dependency
Differentiation	Economies of Scale	Etc.	Switching Costs	Switching Costs
Fixed Costs	Distribution		Product Specialization	Price Sensitivity
Etc.	Brand		Etc.	Etc.
	Etc.			

When to Use—Evaluate the Forces Within Your Industry

Use Porter's Five Forces model to understand the competitive dynamics within an industry, predict changes in competition, influence the evolution of industry structure, and identify strategic positions. The framework helps analyze the forces shaping economic value distribution among industry participants, aiding strategic decision making.

Context and Scenarios of Use

Porter's Five Forces framework is a versatile tool that can be applied in various business scenarios to analyze industry competition. Here are some key examples:

- **Market Entry Decisions:** Companies considering entering a new market can use the framework to assess barriers to entry, the intensity of competition, and the power of suppliers and customers. This helps determine whether the market is attractive or risky.
- **Strategic Planning:** Businesses can apply the Five Forces to identify competitive pressures within their industry and adjust their strategies. For example, if competitive rivalry is high, a firm might focus on differentiating its product. Alternatively, if supplier power is high, a firm might focus on diversifying its suppliers.

- **Investment Analysis:** Investors can use the model to evaluate industries' profitability potential before making investment decisions. By understanding industry forces, they can forecast how these might impact returns. For example, if there are few competitors, the concentration may allow for stable returns unless the threat of new entrants increases.
- **Supplier Negotiations:** Companies facing high supplier power can use the framework to explore alternatives, such as backward integration or finding substitute inputs, to reduce dependence.
- **Industry Disruption Assessment:** Firms can analyze emerging threats from substitutes or new entrants—such as technological disruptions or start-ups—using the Five Forces, enabling proactive adaptation to competitive changes.

In each scenario, Porter's Five Forces framework provides valuable insights into the competitive landscape by analyzing the threat of new entrants, the bargaining power of suppliers and buyers, the threat of substitutes, and the intensity of rivalry within an industry.

How to Use

To implement Porter's Five Forces model, begin by analyzing each of these forces to better understand the competitive pressures in your industry and make informed strategic decisions.

1. **Threat of New Entrants**
    - Evaluate Barriers to Entry: Assess the factors that make it difficult for new competitors to enter the industry. Barriers to entry include capital requirements, economies of scale, access to distribution channels, government regulations, and brand loyalty. Industries with high barriers to entry are less likely to experience new competition, while low barriers can lead to market saturation.
    - Analyze the Potential for New Competitors: Consider the likelihood of new entrants based on the current competitive

environment. If barriers are low, companies need to prepare for potential new competitors who could drive down prices or take market share. Conversely, industries with strong barriers may allow incumbents to enjoy sustained profitability.

2. **Bargaining Power of Buyers**
   - Assess Buyer Concentration and Dependency: The power of buyers increases when they are few in number but purchase large volumes, giving them leverage to demand lower prices or better terms. Conversely, when buyers are fragmented and individual purchases are small, their bargaining power is reduced.
   - Evaluate Switching Costs and Price Sensitivity: If customers can easily switch to a competitor's product or service without significant cost or inconvenience, their bargaining power is higher. On the other hand, if switching costs are high, buyers may have less influence. Additionally, the price sensitivity of buyers impacts their bargaining power—when buyers are highly price sensitive, companies may face pressure to lower prices.

3. **Bargaining Power of Suppliers**
   - Examine Supplier Concentration and Dependency: Supplier power is strong when a few suppliers dominate the market or provide unique inputs critical to the business. In such cases, suppliers can dictate terms, raise prices, or reduce the quality of goods and services. When suppliers are abundant, and their products are commoditized, their power is lower, giving businesses more leverage in negotiations.
   - Assess Input Importance and Switching Costs: Suppliers' bargaining power also depends on how critical their inputs are to the business. The supplier's power increases if a company relies on specialized or high-quality inputs that are not easily replaced. Businesses should also consider how costly or disruptive it would be to switch suppliers, as high switching costs can further increase supplier power.

4. **Threat of Substitute Products or Services**
   - Consider the Availability of Alternatives: The presence of substitute products or services can limit an industry's profitability by placing a ceiling on prices. Companies should evaluate how

easily customers can switch to a substitute product or service that offers similar benefits at a lower price or with better features. Industries with many viable substitutes face greater competitive pressure.

- o Assess Price and Quality of Substitutes: It's not just the availability of substitutes but also their price and performance that matter. If substitutes offer a better price–performance ratio, customers may be more inclined to switch. Companies need to monitor substitutes closely to ensure their offerings remain competitive.

5. **Intensity of Competitive Rivalry**
   - o Evaluate the Number of Competitors and Market Growth: The intensity of rivalry among existing competitors is a key determinant of industry profitability. Rivalry is typically higher in industries with many competitors, slow growth, or limited differentiation. When the industry is growing rapidly, companies can often achieve growth without intense competition; however, competition for market share intensifies when growth slows.
   - o Assess Differentiation and Fixed Costs: The degree of product or service differentiation impacts the intensity of rivalry. In industries where products are highly differentiated, companies can compete on factors other than price, reducing rivalry. Conversely, in sectors where products are commoditized and fixed costs are high, price competition is more common, leading to lower profitability.

Notes for Your Use

- **Gather Information:** Collect data on industry barriers to entry, buyer and supplier concentration, substitutes, and competitive rivalry.
- **Evaluate:** Analyze the strength of each force. Assess barriers to entry, buyer power, supplier power, the availability of substitutes, and the intensity of rivalry. Understand how these forces impact profitability and market dynamics.

- **Connect:** Apply the analysis to your current competitive position. Identify the forces that are most critical to your strategic decisions and where vulnerabilities or opportunities lie.
- **Develop Strategy:** Craft strategies that mitigate the strongest forces. For example, develop strong brand loyalty to reduce buyer power or explore vertical integration to reduce supplier power.
- **Implement Strategy:** Regularly monitor the industry for changes in these forces and adapt strategies to maintain competitiveness.

Industry Profit Pools or Industry Value Chain Analysis

Brief History

In their 1998 article "Profit Pools: A Fresh Look at Strategy," Orit Gadiesh and James Gilbert introduce the concept of profit pools.[50] They define profit pools as the total profits generated across an entire industry, which can vary significantly by segment, product line, or geographic region. Gadiesh and Gilbert argue that while revenues may be concentrated in certain areas, profits often reside elsewhere in the value chain. To maximize profitability, companies must map the industry's profit pool, identify the highest profit margins, and then realign their strategies to focus on these high-profit areas. This approach encourages firms to look beyond traditional revenue metrics and instead prioritize areas that offer greater profitability, often requiring a shift in focus or operations.

Model 39 of 50: Industry Profit Pools
Industry Profit Pools, Value Chain

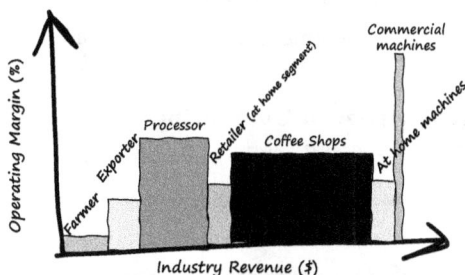

When to Use—Evaluate Where Value Sits Within the Industry

Profit pool analysis is beneficial when a company seeks to understand the distribution of profits within an industry. By mapping profit concentrations, businesses can identify strategic opportunities, allocate resources effectively, and stay ahead of industry shifts. Understanding where the profit sits (and why) allows for focusing on high-profit segments, optimizing competitive positions, and making informed decisions to enhance profitability.

Context and Scenarios of Use

Profit pools are helpful in many contexts when a company aims to understand where profit resides across a complex industry. Here are some scenarios for using profit pools:

- **Industry Restructuring:** A company operating in an industry facing shifts in technology, regulations, or consumer preferences can use profit pool analysis to identify emerging areas of profitability across the industry. This helps reallocate resources to higher-margin segments or move them into the most profitable segments.
- **Expansion into New Markets:** When expanding into a new market or geography, companies can map profit pools to focus on the most profitable areas of the industry rather than simply chasing market share. This approach ensures better financial returns.
- **Strategic Reinvestment:** Companies looking to reinvest earnings into innovation or growth can use profit pool analysis to pinpoint where future profits will likely grow. This can guide R&D or capital investment to areas that promise the highest returns.
- **Vertical Integration or Outsourcing Decisions:** Companies can assess the profitability across the value chain (e.g., production, distribution, and retail) to determine whether vertical integration makes sense or whether certain activities should be outsourced based on profit concentration.

- **Competitive Strategy Adjustments:** Firms facing intense competition in low-margin segments can use profit pool insights to shift focus to less contested, higher-margin areas where competitors are less active, allowing for more profitable differentiation.

By focusing on profit pools, companies can avoid pursuing revenue growth in low-margin areas and instead target areas with the highest potential for profitability.

How to Use

Profit pool analysis involves several steps to identify and understand profit concentrations within an industry:

1. **Define the Pool:** Begin by defining the profit pool, considering the entire value chain from raw materials to the end consumer. Take a broad view of value chain activities without unnecessary disaggregation.
2. **Determine Pool Size:** Estimate the size of the profit pool by developing a baseline of cumulative profits generated across all relevant activities. To get a comprehensive view, look at both company and product levels.
3. **Estimate Profit Distribution:** Break down the total profit pool by estimating profits at each activity level. Shift between aggregate and disaggregate views, considering "pure players" and "mixed players" across multiple pools. Use your company's economics as a reference and capture assumptions for data gaps.
4. **Reconcile Estimates:** Compare the outputs of steps 2 and 3 to ensure consistency. If the numbers don't add up, revisit assumptions, calculations, and data gaps. Collect additional data to fill gaps and resolve inconsistencies.
5. **Assess Movements Across Pools:** Consider industry dynamics, such as Porter's Five Forces, to assess potential movements across profit pools. Understand how external factors may impact the distribution of profits.

6. **Present the Analysis:** Illustrate the profit pools clearly, showcasing current value locations and projecting future movements. Use visualizations or charts to communicate the findings effectively.

By following these steps, you can gain valuable insights into where profits are concentrated within the industry. This information allows you to make informed strategic decisions, allocate resources efficiently, and anticipate shifts in the competitive landscape.

Notes for Your Use

- **Define the Pool:** Identify the profit pool by examining the entire value chain, from raw materials to end consumers, to ensure a broad overview of value chain activities.
- **Determine Pool Size:** Estimate the overall profit pool by analyzing cumulative profits across relevant value chain activities from both company and product perspectives.
- **Estimate Profit Distribution:** Break down the pool and assess profits at each level. Compare "pure" and "mixed players" to gauge profit distribution within various activities.
- **Reconcile Estimates:** Cross-check data and calculations for consistency. Revisit assumptions or gather additional data to resolve discrepancies.
- **Assess Movements Across Pools:** Evaluate market dynamics using tools like Porter's Five Forces to predict potential shifts in profit distribution.
- **Present the Analysis:** Visualize the findings through charts or graphs to illustrate current and future profit concentrations, aiding strategic decisions.

Industry Life Cycle Stages

Brief History

The Industry Life Cycle concept evolved from earlier work on the Product Life Cycle, notably developed by economist Raymond Vernon in his 1966 article, "International Investment and International Trade in the Product

Cycle."[51] Vernon's theory explained how products progress through stages. Building on Vernon's ideas, the Industry Life Cycle expanded this concept to entire industries, recognizing that industries, like products, also experience phases of introduction, growth, shakeout, maturity, and decline.

Model 40 of 50: Industry Life Cycle Stages

Industry Life Cycle

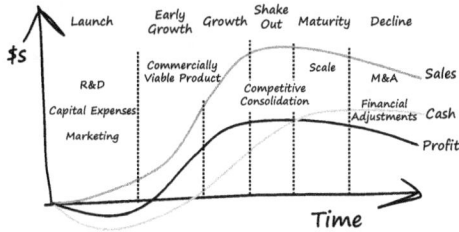

When to Use—Identify the Stage and Determine Actions

Use the industry life cycle framework when assessing the competitive industry landscape and a company's growth potential, profitability, and cash flow generation. By identifying an industry's position in its life cycle—whether in the introduction, growth, maturity, or decline stage—stakeholders can make more informed strategic decisions based on the unique challenges and opportunities associated with each phase. This analysis helps you to navigate the dynamic nature of industries and tailor strategies accordingly.

Context and Scenarios of Use

Industry life cycle analysis provides valuable insights by helping you understand the current stage of your industry and make informed decisions within that stage. The framework is applicable across various scenarios, as detailed below:

- **Strategic Planning and Decision Making:** When a company considers a significant investment in a particular industry, it must assess the industry life cycle stage (e.g., introduction, growth, and maturity) to adjust strategy accordingly. For example, in the growth phase, aggressive investments might be appropriate due to increasing demand and profitability. At the same time, in the decline stage, the company may pursue niche markets or prepare an exit strategy.

- **Market Entry Strategy:** A start-up entering a new market can leverage industry life cycle analysis to determine the best approach. If the industry is in the introduction stage, the start-up should build awareness, educate customers, and gain early adopters. In the growth phase, the company's strategy might shift toward product differentiation and rapid scaling to capture market share.

- **International Expansion:** Companies exploring international markets can apply industry life cycle analysis to assess industry maturity across different regions. By identifying regions where the industry is still in the growth stage, firms can capitalize on opportunities for rapid expansion. Conversely, mature or declining industries may require tailored entry strategies or even avoidance.

- **Investment and Portfolio Management:** Private equity firms and investors can use industry life cycle analysis to guide investment decisions. Industries in the growth or early maturity stages typically present higher profitability, making them more attractive to investors. Conversely, declining industries may only appeal to those seeking turnaround opportunities or particular situations.

- **Mergers & Acquisitions (M&A):** Companies evaluating acquisition targets can use industry life cycle analysis to identify industries in the shakeout or maturity stages, where consolidation is common. During these phases, stronger competitors are likely to acquire weaker ones. The industry life cycle analysis aids in identifying acquisition opportunities that may result in competitive advantages or partnerships.

- **Innovation and R&D Investment:** A technology company deciding on R&D expenditure can rely on ILC analysis to allocate resources effectively. In the introduction or early growth stages, heavy investment in R&D is often necessary to innovate and stay ahead of competitors. In contrast, during the maturity stage, R&D efforts may shift toward incremental improvements and cost efficiencies.

By aligning corporate strategies with the appropriate stage of the industry life cycle, you can anticipate industry-specific challenges and capitalize on emerging opportunities. Industry life cycle analysis is an essential tool for comprehensive strategic decision making.

How to Use

To strategically navigate the industry life cycle, you must first identify their position on the life cycle curve, which typically consists of five stages: Launch, Growth, Shakeout, Maturity, and Decline. Once this stage is determined, you can follow these key steps to align their strategies with the challenges and opportunities of each phase:

1. **Launch Stage**
   - **Focus on R&D and Product-Market Fit:** In the introduction phase of an industry, businesses should prioritize R&D to innovate and bring new products or services to market. Securing product-market fit is crucial, as it will set the foundation for future growth. Capital should be allocated heavily toward R&D and initial marketing to build awareness and attract early adopters.
   - **Low Regulation:** At this stage, industries often experience minimal regulatory oversight since the regulatory environment has not yet caught up with the emerging market. Companies can leverage this regulatory gap to rapidly test and introduce new offerings before rules become more stringent.
2. **Growth Stage (Early Growth and Growth)**
   - **Establish Commercial Viability:** As demand increases, businesses must demonstrate the commercial potential of their products or services. This involves scaling operations, expanding production, and ensuring that the business model is profitable and sustainable over the long term.

- ○ **Competitive Landscape:** With rapid growth comes increased competition as new entrants enter the market to capture a share of the growing demand. Companies must focus on differentiating themselves from competitors through innovation, branding, and superior customer service.
- ○ **Regulatory Awareness:** As the industry gains recognition and becomes more established, regulatory oversight tends to increase. Businesses need to stay proactive, anticipating regulatory changes and ensuring compliance to avoid disruptions to their operations.

3. **Shakeout Stage**
   - ○ **Regulatory Catchup:** During this phase, industries typically face a surge in regulatory measures as authorities gain a deeper understanding of the industry. Compliance becomes a priority as businesses must adapt to stricter regulations.
   - ○ **Competition Consolidation:** As competition intensifies, weaker companies often exit the market, while stronger players consolidate their positions through mergers and acquisitions. Companies that differentiate themselves through innovation, operational efficiency, or superior customer experience will likely emerge as industry leaders. M&A activity accelerates as market players seek to expand their capabilities or acquire competitors.

4. **Maturity Stage**
   - ○ **Stable Margins and Cash Flow:** In the maturity stage, industries tend to experience stable profit margins and reliable cash flows. The focus shifts from rapid growth to operational efficiency, optimizing capital structure, and maintaining profitability. Companies may seek to reduce costs, increase productivity, or expand into adjacent markets to sustain their position.
   - ○ **Industry Concentration:** Industry concentration tends to increase as market share becomes concentrated in fewer dominant players. This is often a result of mergers, acquisitions, or the exit of smaller competitors. With surplus cash flow, companies may invest in technology upgrades, pursue further acquisitions, or return capital to shareholders.

5. **Decline Stage**
   - **Strategic Choices:** As demand diminishes, businesses face strategic decisions about their future. Companies may choose to reinvent themselves by diversifying into new markets or product lines, or they may opt to return capital to shareholders through dividends or stock buybacks.
   - **Mergers and Acquisitions:** M&A activity plays a critical role, as companies in declining industries often seek growth through acquisitions. This consolidates the remaining market share among a few key players, leading to higher revenue concentration within the industry.
   - **Financial Engineering:** Companies may rely on financial engineering tactics, such as share repurchases or restructuring, to boost shareholder value without organic growth opportunities. These strategies are often employed when growth prospects are limited, and the focus shifts to managing financial metrics.

By understanding and leveraging the dynamics of each stage in the Industry Life Cycle, you can tailor your strategies to align with the unique challenges and opportunities of the stage. This ensures a more informed approach to competition, market trends, and regulatory changes, ultimately driving long-term success.

Notes for Your Use

- **Gather Information:** Collect data on industry investments, sales, cash, and profit trends.
- **Evaluate:** Discuss the industry life cycle stage in which the industry is operating.
- **Connect:** Connect the industry with your company's operating investments, sales, cash, and profit trends to confirm the stage.
- **Develop Strategy:** Develop a strategy based on the industry life cycle stage.
- **Implement Strategy:** Implement and evaluate with an understanding that the stages change over time. Look ahead to future stage changes.

ADL Matrix

Brief History

The ADL Matrix, developed by Arthur D. Little, Inc., was first published in the late 1970s. It offers a two-dimensional analysis for evaluating a company's businesses or business units based on the industry life cycle stage and competitive position. The matrix is designed to help organizations improve their business portfolio and overall strategic management.

Model 41 of 50: ADL Matrix

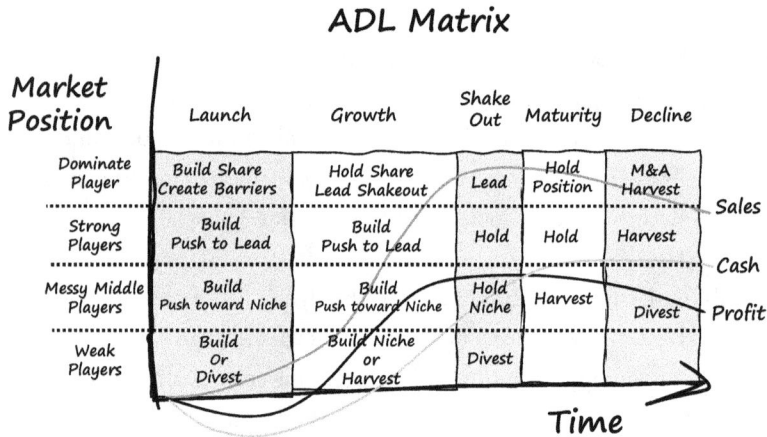

When to Use—Evaluate How Market Position Impacts Actions Across the Industry Life Cycle

The ADL Matrix is beneficial in strategic planning for business units. It excels in aligning competitive position strategies with various stages of the industry life cycle. By linking to the industry life cycle, the matrix aids in tailoring strategies based on each stage's specific challenges and opportunities, ensuring effective decision making and resource allocation.

Context and Scenarios of Use

The ADL Matrix is a versatile analytical tool employed in various contexts for strategic decision making and business portfolio management. It assists you in understanding your strategic positioning and guiding future actions. The following sections outline vital contexts and scenarios in which the ADL Matrix can be effectively utilized:

- **Strategic Planning:** The ADL Matrix is valuable during strategic planning sessions. Organizations can evaluate their portfolio of businesses by assessing each line's competitive position and industry life cycle stage. This evaluation enables companies to identify which businesses require further investment, innovation, or potential divestment.
- **Resource Allocation:** Effective resource allocation is critical for organizational success. The ADL Matrix aids companies in making informed decisions about where to direct limited resources. Organizations may choose to prioritize investments in strong businesses within growing industries while considering reducing investments in weaker units that operate in declining markets.
- **Market Entry Strategy:** The ADL Matrix provides valuable insights when considering entering new markets or launching new businesses. Firms evaluating entry into emerging markets can analyze the competitive landscape and the life cycle stage. This analysis allows organizations to determine which opportunities align best with their strengths and strategic objectives.
- **Mergers and Acquisitions (M&A):** The ADL Matrix is instrumental in assessing potential acquisition targets. Companies seeking to acquire other firms can evaluate the target organization's competitive position and industry life cycle stage. This evaluation helps align acquisition decisions with broader strategic objectives and assesses the target's fit within the company's existing portfolio.
- **Divestiture Decisions:** The ADL Matrix assists companies in determining when to divest or discontinue specific product lines or business units. Suppose a business unit is in a declining industry with a weak competitive position. In that case, the matrix can indicate that divestiture is a viable strategy, enabling the reallocation of resources to more promising opportunities.

- **Scenario Planning:** Organizations can utilize the ADL Matrix in scenario planning to anticipate potential changes in the industry landscape. By analyzing how shifts in technology or consumer behavior could impact product life cycle stages, businesses can adjust their strategies proactively to remain competitive.

Businesses gain valuable insights into their strategic positioning by leveraging the ADL Matrix across these various contexts and scenarios. This analytical tool enhances understanding of the competitive landscape and facilitates effective portfolio management, allowing you to make informed decisions aligning with their objectives.

How to Use

To use the ADL Matrix in developing a strategy, follow these steps:

1. **Identify Business Units Through Which Your Organization Operates:** Clearly define the business unit boundaries and determine which to analyze using the ADL Matrix. If you are conducting a portfolio analysis, identify all business units.
2. **Assess Industry Life Cycle Stage:** Determine the current stage of the industry life cycle for each identified business unit. The stages typically include introduction, growth, maturity, and decline. For more details on assessing the life cycle, use the industry life cycle analysis tool.
3. **Determine Competitive Position:** Evaluate each unit's competitive position within its industry. This involves assessing market share, profitability, and competitive advantage. For more details on conducting competitor analysis, turn to the competitor section.
4. **Plot Units on the Matrix:** Use the ADL Matrix to plot each business unit based on its industry life cycle stage and competitive position. This positioning provides a visual representation of the portfolio.

5. **Define Strategies for Each Quadrant:** Develop specific strategies for business units in each quadrant of the matrix. For example:
   - *Build*: Invest resources to enhance and strengthen businesses in the growth phase.
   - *Hold*: Maintain a stable business position in the mature phase, focusing on efficiency and optimization.
   - *Harvest*: Extract maximum cash flow from businesses in the decline phase, considering cost reduction and divestiture.
   - *Divest*: Exit or divest businesses with low market share and limited growth prospects.

6. **Allocate Resources:** Allocate resources according to the defined strategies. This involves directing investments, marketing efforts, and operational focus in alignment with the strategic goals for each business unit.

7. **Periodic Review and Adjustment:** Regularly review and adjust the positioning and strategies on the ADL Matrix. Industries and business competitive positions evolve, requiring ongoing assessment and adaptation of the strategic approach.

By systematically applying the ADL Matrix, you can optimize your portfolio management, allocate resources effectively, and navigate the dynamic landscape of different industry life cycle stages.

Notes for Your Use

- **Gather Information:** Identify the business units within your organization to analyze using the ADL Matrix for portfolio analysis.
- **Evaluate Industry Life Cycle Stage:** Determine the current industry life cycle stage for each business unit (introduction, growth, maturity, decline).
- **Determine Competitive Position:** Assess each unit's competitive position based on market share, profitability, and competitive advantage.

- **Plot Units on the Matrix:** Use the ADL Matrix to visually represent each business unit according to its life cycle stage and competitive position.
- **Define Strategies for Each Quadrant:** Develop specific strategies for each quadrant.
- **Allocate Resources:** Direct investments, marketing efforts, and operational focus according to the defined strategies for each unit.
- **Periodic Review and Adjustment:** Regularly assess and adapt positioning and strategies on the ADL Matrix to stay aligned with industry and competitive changes.

Climate Checklist

The final model serves as a structured guide, organizing the discussion and linking to models in Section 5. As you go through the checklist, dive deep into understanding the climate your organization operates within, the external cultural forces, the geopolitical forces, the competitive landscape, the industry value, and the life cycle. Consider framing your business within these externalities to create an advantage.

Start by analyzing cultural differences if you are operating across a diverse multinational landscape. How can you minimize the impacts of these forces? Then, expand to the geopolitical, social, economic, legal, and technical differences across the areas where you are operating or plan to operate. Finally, link to the national advantages where you are operating or plan to operate. Do you have an advantage or disadvantage?

Next, assess the climate with closer proximity to your organization. Identify the suppliers, customers, competitors, and new entrants entwined with your operation. What are the competitive dynamics across the different players? Do you have an advantage or disadvantage?

Drive one step deeper into your value chain by understanding where value sits across the industry in which you operate. Do you sit where the most significant value accrues, or do you have the advantage to gain value elsewhere across the chain?

Once you understand the value, assess the life cycle of your industry and your competitive position to determine future moves that allow you to gain value over time.

By following this checklist and thoroughly analyzing your climate, you can develop strategies that navigate or disrupt the broader landscape within your industry. This will allow your business to grow in value over time.

Model 42 of 50: Climate Checklist

Question	Tools	Your team's thoughts
How could the broad environment landscape change	CAGE PESTEL	
What country/region advantages exist? Can they change?	Porter's Diamond	
How could industry dynamics change?	Porter's 5 Forces	
How could industry value move?	Profit Pools Value Chain	
How has and could the industry evolve?	Industry Life Cycle ADL Matrix	

SECTION 6

Consolidation: Pulling Everything Together

In the Consolidation phase, the focus shifts to synthesizing insights gained from previous sections to define a cohesive strategic direction. Building on the foundational understanding established in the 5 Cs (Company, Characteristics, Customers and Collaborators, Competitors, and Climate), this phase evaluates internal strengths and weaknesses, product value propositions, customer segments, competitive dynamics, and external market forces. By systematically analyzing these areas, the organization identifies synergies, trade-offs, and strategic priorities to inform impactful implementation.

The Consolidation "C" models provide various frameworks for integrating insights across the 5 Cs into a unified strategy. Early models in the Consolidation section help determine the ultimate unifying strategy that your organization should consider using varying methodologies. For example, SPACE Analysis assesses the organization's Financial Strength, Competitive Advantage, Industry Strength, and Environmental Stability to identify the optimal strategic posture. Attack and Defense Strategies offer specific methods to pursue growth or protect assets in competitive markets. Lafley and Martin's 5-Step Strategy organizes planning around core strategic elements, from defining aspirations to aligning resources effectively. Mintzberg's 5 Ps of Strategy introduces flexibility by combining deliberate planning with adaptability, considering five perspectives to balance strategic intent. Ohmae's 3Cs Model focuses on aligning company strengths with customer needs and competitive positioning, while Porter's Generic Strategies advocate for a singular focus—Cost Leadership, Differentiation, or Focus—to sharpen competitive advantage. Hambrick and Fredrickson's Strategy Diamond structures strategy around five interconnected elements, creating a framework for execution. Finally, the

Emergent Strategy model emphasizes adaptability, with a guiding principle that evolves in response to market changes.

Together, these models consolidate the 5 Cs into a strategy that aligns internal strengths with external opportunities, ensuring resilience and sustainable competitive advantage in an ever-changing market landscape.

To begin this section, start with the outcomes from the previous five C's. The checklist at the end of each section is the best tool for beginning Section 6.

The questions you and your team should discuss and align upon as you enter the Consolidation stage:

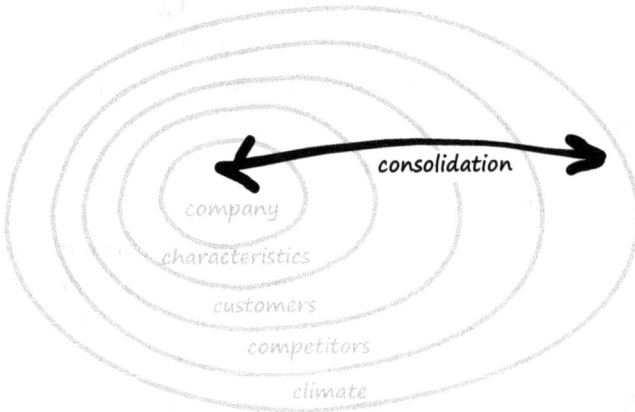

Company
- *What is our competitive advantage?*
- *How is our competitive advantage sustainable?*
- *How are we organized around our competitive advantage?*
- *What opportunities exist to leverage our competitive advantage?*
- *What are the threats to our competitive advantage?*
- *How are we prepared to mitigate these threats?*

Characteristics

- Who buys from us today, and who do we want to buy from us tomorrow? Are these different?
- What are we offering these customers?
- Where are our products and services in their evolution? New or old to the customers?
- Who are the vital few—products and customers? What do we really care about?
- What are our break-even points? Do we measure them?
- What is the most resilient part of our portfolio? What is least?

Customers & Collaborators

- How are we helping customers with jobs or services?
- What are the customers' needs or pain points?
- How are the customers similar and dissimilar?
- What is the value of our customers?
- How are we aligned with other parties?

Competitors

- How competitively intensive is our industry?
- What drives our competitors' actions?
- How do we perform versus our competitors?
- What are the competitive groupings and barriers?
- Are we staying ahead in the race?
- Can we change the structure with cooperation?

Climate
- *How could the broad environment landscape change?*
- *What country/region advantages exist? Can they change?*
- *How could industry dynamics change?*
- *How could industry value change?*
- *How has and could the industry evolve?*
- *How has the industry evolved?*
- *How can the industry change in the future?*

SPACE Analysis

Brief History

The SPACE model is often attributed to the methods in *Strategic Management: A Methodological Approach,* coauthored by Rowe et al.[52] Their research in strategic methodologies provides a structured way for organizations to evaluate their strategic posture based on financial strength, competitive advantage, industry strength, and environmental stability. This allows them to take appropriate strategic actions based on a visual representation of these factors.

Model 43 of 50: SPACE Analysis

SPACE Analysis

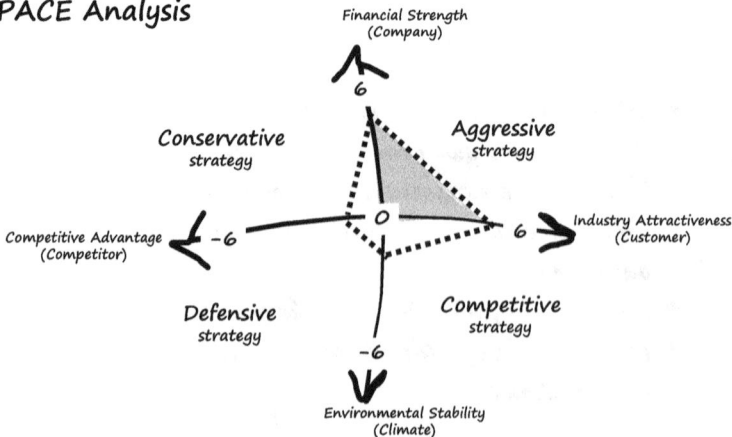

When to Use—Assess the Prior 5 Cs to Create a Consolidated Strategy

SPACE Analysis is beneficial when you seek strategic broad alignment between internal capabilities and external market dynamics. Employ this model when crafting strategies to ensure they harmonize with the prevailing business environment. It offers a structured framework for evaluating internal and external risks, enabling proactive identification and mitigation of potential challenges. Use the SPACE model during strategic planning to enhance decision making, foster adaptability, and position the organization for success by aligning its strengths with market opportunities while addressing potential weaknesses and threats.

How to Use

The SPACE model is a strategic management tool that aids decision making by evaluating internal and external factors. It utilizes a matrix diagram with two internal (Financial Strength and Competitive Advantage) and two external (Environmental Stability and Industry Attractiveness) dimensions, resulting in four areas for analysis.

To score the matrix, assign values between 0 and 6 for Financial Strength and Industry Attractiveness and between −6 and 0 for Competitive Advantage and Environmental Stability. Higher scores indicate a favorable position for the former, while lower scores indicate strength for the latter. Average scores for each area are then plotted on the matrix. Use the prior 5 Cs of your analysis to complete the assessment.

Interpretation involves determining the quadrant with the largest area covered by the plotted points. Based on the company's position on these axes, there are **four strategic outcomes: Aggressive, Conservative, Defensive,** and **Competitive.** These strategic outcomes are the Consolidation. Here's a detailed breakdown of each:

1. **Aggressive Strategy (example in the model above)**
   - **When to Use:** This outcome is suitable when a company has strong financial strength and a competitive advantage in a stable industry and environment.

- ○ **Characteristics**:
  - High profitability, strong cash flow, and sufficient resources.
  - The company enjoys advantages over competitors, such as market leadership, superior products, or operational efficiencies.
  - The industry is stable, with predictable market demand and low volatility.
- ○ **Strategic Focus:**
  - **Growth and Expansion**: The company is well-positioned to pursue aggressive expansion strategies, such as entering new markets, increasing market share, or acquiring competitors.
  - **Investment in R&D**: The firm may invest heavily in innovation, new technologies, and product development to further strengthen its competitive position.
  - **Market Penetration**: Focus on increasing sales within existing markets, launching aggressive marketing campaigns, or enhancing distribution channels.
- ○ **Examples:**
  - Expanding operations into new regions or countries.
  - Launching new product lines or services to capture additional customer segments.
  - Mergers and acquisitions to increase market dominance.

2. **Conservative Strategy**
   - ○ **When to Use**: A conservative strategy is ideal when a company operates in a stable environment but lacks either financial strength or a competitive advantage.
   - ○ **Characteristics**:
     - The external environment is relatively predictable, but the company may face resource limitations or operational inefficiencies.
     - The business may have a modest market share and profitability or face strong competition.
   - ○ **Strategic Focus:**
     - **Preserve and Protect**: The company's priority is to maintain its current position rather than risk aggressive expansion.

- **Cost Efficiency**: Focus on improving operational efficiency, reducing costs, and optimizing internal processes.
- **Selective Investment**: The firm should make cautious, targeted investments in areas that will strengthen core operations or marginally expand market reach.
- **Defensive Positioning**: Protecting market share in stable areas and avoiding overextension in high-risk areas.

○ **Examples:**
  - Focusing on core competencies and reinforcing customer relationships.
  - Streamlining operations to improve efficiency without heavy spending.
  - Incremental innovations or small-scale improvements to products or services.

3. **Defensive Strategy**
   ○ **When to Use**: A defensive strategy is necessary when a company is in a weak financial position and operates in an unstable, competitive industry or a volatile environment.
   ○ **Characteristics:**
     - The company may struggle with low profitability, declining market share, or high operational costs.
     - The industry is highly competitive or experiencing rapid change, creating additional challenges for survival.
   ○ **Strategic Focus:**
     - **Retrenchment and Cost-Cutting**: The primary focus is on cost reductions, reducing overhead, and focusing on the most profitable areas of the business.
     - **Divestment**: Consider selling non-core or underperforming assets to strengthen the balance sheet.
     - **Narrow Focus**: Concentrate resources on key business areas, scaling back operations or market presence where necessary.
     - **Survival Mode**: The focus is on maintaining liquidity and financial stability rather than pursuing growth.

- ○ **Examples:**
  - ▪ Exiting unprofitable markets or discontinuing underperforming product lines.
  - ▪ Restructuring the organization, downsizing, or laying off staff.
  - ▪ Reducing investment in R&D, marketing, or expansion to conserve cash flow.

4. **Competitive Strategy**
   - ○ **When to Use:** A competitive strategy is appropriate when a company has strong financial strength but operates in a volatile or competitive industry.
   - ○ **Characteristics:**
     - ▪ The firm has the financial capacity to pursue strategic moves but faces significant competitive pressure or operates in a fast-changing, dynamic industry.
     - ▪ The industry may experience high rates of innovation, technological change, or rapidly shifting customer demands.
   - ○ **Strategic Focus:**
     - ▪ **Innovation and Differentiation:** The company should focus on differentiating its offerings from competitors through innovation, product quality, or superior customer service.
     - ▪ **Selective Expansion:** The firm can pursue growth but must be cautious, focusing on areas where it has a clear advantage or sees high potential.
     - ▪ **Proactive Competition:** The company should actively compete through tactics like marketing, product launches, or strategic partnerships, capitalizing on opportunities before competitors.
     - ▪ **Adaptability:** The firm needs to be agile and flexible to respond to changes in the market or competitive landscape.
   - ○ **Examples:**
     - ▪ Developing new products or services that are significantly different from competitors' offerings.
     - ▪ Using advanced technology, R&D, or customer insights to create unique value propositions.
     - ▪ Engaging in strategic alliances or partnerships to enhance capabilities or market reach.

The SPACE model provides a visual representation of an organization's strategic position, facilitating informed decision making based on its unique market circumstances and competitive landscape.

Notes for Your Use

- **Gather Information:** Utilize the 5 Cs framework to collect data on internal strengths, product value propositions, customer segments, competitive landscapes, and external market forces.
- **Evaluate:** Use the SPACE model to assess Financial Strength, Competitive Advantage, Environmental Stability, and Industry Attractiveness, scoring each dimension to determine the organization's strategic position.
- **Connect:** Plot the average scores on the SPACE matrix to visualize the strategic position and identify the quadrant with the largest area covered.
- **Develop Strategy:** Based on the quadrant position, determine the appropriate strategy (Aggressive, Conservative, Defensive, or Competitive) and outline specific strategic focuses for each.
- **Implement Strategy:** Allocate resources according to the determined strategies that are regularly reviewed and adjusted based on market conditions and competitive dynamics.

Attack and Defense Strategy Plan

Brief History

Jorge Vasconcellos e Sá's work in *Strategy Moves: 14 Complete Attack and Defense Strategies for Competitive Advantage* offers a structured approach to how companies can compete effectively in dynamic markets.[53] His strategies draw from military principles but are adapted to business contexts. Vasconcellos emphasizes that strategy is not just about outsmarting competitors but also about timing, positioning, and adapting based on the competitive landscape, which results in maneuvers similar to those employed by military units

Model 44 of 50: Attack and Defense Strategy

Attack & Defense Strategy Plan

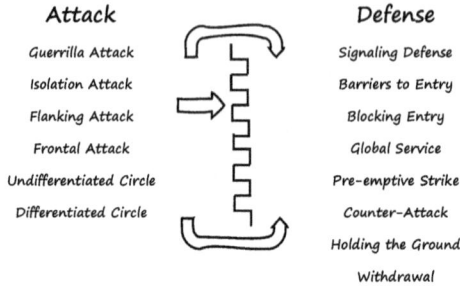

Attack		Defense
Guerrilla Attack		Signaling Defense
Isolation Attack		Barriers to Entry
Flanking Attack		Blocking Entry
Frontal Attack		Global Service
Undifferentiated Circle		Pre-emptive Strike
Differentiated Circle		Counter-Attack
		Holding the Ground
		Withdrawal

When to Use—Assess the Prior 5 Cs to Develop Your Strategic Plan

Attack and defense strategy concepts offer a structured approach to navigating competitive markets. Attack strategies are useful when you aim to enter new markets, grow aggressively, or exploit competitor weaknesses, driving market share and innovation. These are most effective in high-growth markets or when competitors are vulnerable. On the other hand, defense strategies are key when you are looking to protect their existing market positions, core assets, and profitability in the face of competitive threats. They are particularly valuable in saturated, mature, or volatile markets. These concepts also guide resource allocation—determining whether to invest in expansion or focus on protecting strengths.

How to Use

By understanding when to attack or defend, you can adapt your strategies to changing market dynamics, ensuring both long-term growth and sustainability. Ultimately, these frameworks provide strategic flexibility to respond effectively to external pressures and opportunities. To effectively apply attack and defense strategies, you should integrate detailed analysis across the 5 Cs. Consider these aspects in your evaluation:

1. **Market Condition Analysis:**
   - **Growth Stage**: Identify whether the market is growing, mature, or declining.

- In high-growth markets (both in unit growth and value growth), there is room to capture more market share so that companies can use aggressive attack strategies like frontal, flanking, or bypass attacks.
- In mature or saturated markets, growth is limited, and competition is fierce, so defense strategies like position or flanking defense are more relevant.

○ **Customer Needs**: Understand shifts in customer preferences or unmet needs. Attack strategies can exploit unmet demands in high-growth or underserved segments.

2. **Competitor Analysis:**

○ **Competitor Strengths and Weaknesses**: Conduct a SWOT (Strengths, Weaknesses, Opportunities, Threats) analysis of key competitors.

- If a competitor has weaknesses (e.g., poor customer service, outdated technology), consider flanking or guerrilla attacks to exploit these gaps.
- If competitors are strong and entrenched, focusing on defensive strategies, such as position defense, may be the best way to maintain your core market share.

○ **Competitor Vulnerabilities**: If competitors are overly focused on traditional markets or technologies and slow to adapt to new trends, bypass attacks can be used.

3. **Resource and Capability Assessment:**

○ **Financial Resources**: Attack strategies, especially frontal or encirclement attacks, require significant financial resources to sustain.

- Ensure you have the necessary capital for sustained campaigns, whether through pricing, marketing, or R&D efforts. If resources are limited, consider guerrilla or defensive strategies.

○ **Operational Capacity**: Attack strategies often require strong supply chains, production capacity, or logistics networks to match or exceed competitors. Defense strategies require less capital but focus on optimizing operations in core areas.

○ **Innovation**: If your company excels in innovation, a bypass attack (introducing disruptive technologies or new business models) may be effective in avoiding head-on competition with incumbents.

4. **Business Goal Alignment:**
   - **Strategic Objectives:** Clearly define your company's strategic goals.
     - If your goal is market leadership, frontal or encirclement attacks might be appropriate to aggressively challenge competitors.
     - If your objective is to maintain profitability or protect a dominant position, position defense or flanking defense helps protect core assets without overextending.
   - **Risk Tolerance:** Attack strategies typically involve higher risk but can lead to rapid market share gains. Defense strategies, by contrast, are more conservative and help sustain stability in volatile environments.

5. **Monitor and Adapt:**
   - **Competitive Responses:** After implementing a strategy, continuously monitor competitor actions. If competitors counter your attack with strong resistance, be prepared to shift from attack to defense, or vice versa.
   - **Market Evolution:** As markets evolve, a company must adapt its strategy. For example, a company might begin with a flanking attack to target underserved segments but then adopt a position defense as it gains dominance in those areas.
   - **Innovation and Change:** Stay agile to capitalize on technological or regulatory shifts. While an attack strategy might be necessary to disrupt the market, as the company grows, it may need to pivot to a defensive strategy to protect its lead.

6. **Strategic Flexibility:**
   - **Hybrid Approaches:** In certain cases, companies might need to combine attack and defense strategies. For example, you may defend your core business while using an attack strategy to enter new markets or niches.
   - **Scenario Planning:** Develop contingency plans for potential competitor responses or market shifts. If a competitor launches an aggressive attack, having a defense strategy ready will ensure you can respond quickly without losing market share.

By aligning your business's capabilities, resources, market conditions, and strategic goals, you can effectively choose and apply the right combination of attack and defense strategies to achieve competitive advantage.

Adapt the strategy to achieve your competitive advantage:

Attack Strategies

1. **Guerrilla Attack**: Utilize low-cost marketing techniques like viral campaigns or social media engagement to reach niche markets. This could involve grassroots promotions or leveraging influencers to gain traction without a large budget.

2. **Isolation Attack:** Identify underserved or overlooked market segments and tailor products specifically for them. Conduct market research to understand their unique needs and preferences, then create specialized marketing messages that resonate with these groups.

3. **Flanking Attack:** Analyze competitors' weaknesses and develop offerings that exploit these vulnerabilities. For example, if a competitor has a strong presence in a premium segment, a company might introduce a budget-friendly alternative targeting value-conscious consumers.

4. **Frontal Attack:** Launch a direct challenge against a competitor's product by offering a superior alternative, emphasizing better features, lower prices, or enhanced customer service. This often involves heavy marketing to position the new product as a better choice.

5. **Undifferentiated Circle:** Create a basic product that appeals to a wide audience, focusing on essential features at a competitive price. Use broad-reaching advertising strategies, such as TV commercials or mass media advertising, to attract a large customer base.

6. **Differentiated Circle:** Implementation: Develop multiple product variations tailored to different market segments. Conduct segmentation analysis to understand distinct customer needs and customize marketing strategies to address each segment effectively.

Defense Strategies

7. **Signaling Defense**: Use public statements or marketing campaigns to communicate a company's strategic intentions, such as announcing future innovations or expansions that may deter competitors from attacking.
8. **Creating Barriers to Entry:** Invest in technologies or processes that create high barriers for new entrants, such as proprietary technologies or exclusive supplier contracts. Use patents or legal protections to safeguard unique aspects of the business model.
9. **Global Service:** Expand operations internationally to create a global footprint, which can deter competition by leveraging economies of scale. This could include establishing partnerships with local distributors or entering joint ventures.
10. **Pre-emptive Strike:** Introduce new products or features before competitors have a chance to react. This requires market intelligence and rapid development cycles to ensure the company is first to market.
11. **Blocking Entry:** Enhance customer loyalty programs or create exclusive partnerships with key suppliers, making it difficult for new entrants to compete. This can involve signing long-term contracts that lock in customers or resources.
12. **Counter-Attack:** Develop a strategic response to competitor actions, such as a price drop or new product launch. This might include adjusting pricing, enhancing features, or increasing promotional efforts to reclaim lost market share.
13. **Holding the Ground:** Reinforce brand loyalty through customer engagement strategies, such as excellent customer service, loyalty rewards, or community involvement. Regularly solicit customer feedback to adapt offerings and maintain satisfaction.
14. **Withdrawal:** Analyze underperforming segments and determine the feasibility of exiting these markets. This involves careful assessment of costs versus benefits and may require a phased withdrawal to minimize negative impacts on brand reputation.

Notes for Your Use

- **Gather Information:** Conduct a market condition analysis to identify the growth stage, customer needs, and shifts in preferences. Use a SWOT analysis to assess competitor strengths and weaknesses.
- **Evaluate:** Analyze resource and capability assessments, focusing on financial resources, operational capacity, and innovation potential. Align strategic objectives and risk tolerance with business goals.
- **Connect:** Monitor and adapt to competitive responses and market evolution, ensuring agility in strategy implementation. Consider strategic flexibility and hybrid approaches to combine attack and defense strategies.
- **Develop Strategy:** Based on market conditions and resource capabilities, choose appropriate attack strategies (e.g., frontal, flanking, encirclement, guerrilla, bypass). Identify defense strategies (e.g., position, mobile, flanking, contraction) to protect market share.
- **Implement Strategy:** Execute selected attack or defense strategies while continuously monitoring competitor actions and market dynamics, adapting as necessary to maintain competitive advantage.

Lafley and Martin's 5-Step Strategy Model

Brief History

A.G. Lafley and Roger Martin introduced the 5-Step Strategy Model in their book *Playing to Win: How Strategy Really Works*.[54] They describe strategy as a "coordinated and integrated set of choices" (p. 5). The model comprises five interconnected steps or choices: (1) Define Your Winning Aspiration: Establishing a clear vision of success; (2) Where to Play: Identifying target markets and segments; (3) How to Win: Crafting a unique value proposition and competitive advantage; (4) Core Capabilities: Recognizing and building the essential strengths needed for execution;

and (5) Management Systems: Implementing the processes and metrics to support the strategy. These choices occur at both the top level of the organization and are nested across subordinate levels in decision making throughout the organization.

Model 45 of 50: 5-Step Strategy Model

Lafley and Martin's 5 Step Strategy model

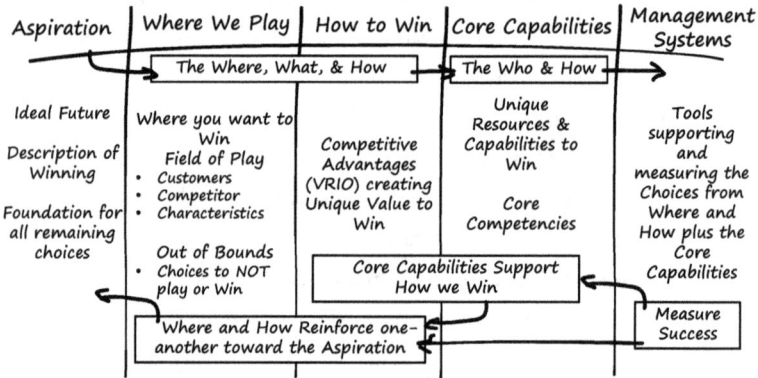

Aspiration	Where We Play	How to Win	Core Capabilities	Management Systems
	The Where, What, & How		The Who & How	
Ideal Future	Where you want to Win	Competitive Advantages (VRIO) creating Unique Value to Win	Unique Resources & Capabilities to Win	Tools supporting and measuring the Choices from Where and How plus the Core Capabilities
Description of Winning	Field of Play • Customers • Competitor • Characteristics		Core Competencies	
Foundation for all remaining choices		Core Capabilities Support How we Win		
	Out of Bounds • Choices to NOT play or Win			
	Where and How Reinforce one-another toward the Aspiration			Measure Success

When to Use—Integrating Your 5 Cs to Build a Game Plan

The 5-Step Strategy Model acts as a consolidation approach that systematically addresses the five crucial steps in an interconnected process—(1) defining winning aspirations, (2) selecting target markets, (3) determining competitive advantage, (4) identifying necessary capabilities, and (5) establishing supportive management systems. The model guides your strategy creation linking elements across the five areas by completing each step. The model utilizes content from the prior 5 Cs to design an integrated approach.

How to Use

To apply Lafley and Martin's model, consider addressing the questions with a view across the prior 5 Cs.

1. **Winning Aspiration:**
   - The aspiration should be practical, rooted in a deep understanding of the company's values and purpose.

- Ensure it creates a shared vision that resonates throughout the organization, inspiring both leadership and employees to pursue long-term success.
- The aspiration should also evolve over time as markets and opportunities change, allowing for innovation and growth.

2. **Where to Play:**
   - This decision must be grounded in detailed market analysis, evaluating not just customer demographics but also competitors, industry trends, and disruptive forces that could affect chosen markets.
   - Consider multiple dimensions such as product categories, distribution channels, or emerging technologies that align with the company's strengths.
   - Regularly reassess the "Where to Play" decisions to ensure the company can pivot quickly if the market or consumer needs change.

3. **How to Win:**
   - Define a clear and differentiated value proposition that sets the company apart from competitors. This could focus on superior product quality, customer experience, innovation, or cost leadership.
   - "How to Win" must also involve not just strategic differentiation but a deep understanding of how the company can leverage its internal strengths, capabilities, and partnerships to win consistently.
   - Factor in scalability and adaptability—how the strategy will evolve as markets mature or shift.

4. **Core Capabilities:**
   - Dive deeper into understanding what truly drives competitive advantage. These can include unique operational processes, advanced R&D, agile supply chains, or brand equity.
   - Prioritize investments in developing and maintaining these core capabilities to sharpen the competitive edge.
   - Identify and address any capability gaps through internal development, external partnerships, acquisitions, or hiring.

5. **Management Systems:**
   - Establish clear metrics that track progress toward the Winning Aspiration and the effectiveness of each strategic decision.
   - Use real-time data and feedback loops to adjust strategies quickly when needed, ensuring the organization remains agile.
   - Embed a culture of continuous improvement by aligning management systems with performance reviews, employee incentives, and organizational learning.

Interconnectedness:

- Each pillar in the "Playing to Win" framework should not be treated in isolation but rather as part of an interconnected system. The "Winning Aspiration" influences the scope of "Where to Play," and decisions on "How to Win" must be supported by appropriate core capabilities.
- Feedback from the "Management Systems" should inform ongoing refinements in strategy, ensuring a dynamic approach that can adapt to new challenges and opportunities.
- Finally, building a strategy that incorporates feedback from frontline employees and customers ensures the organization stays aligned with market realities and operational execution.

Expanding on these elements provides a more comprehensive application of the "Playing to Win" model, ensuring it is not only a theoretical framework but also a practical, actionable guide to achieving sustainable success.

Notes for Your Use

- **Gather Information:** Formulate a winning aspiration aligned with company values by analyzing product offers, customer demographics, competitors, collaborators, and the market climate.
- **Evaluate:** Define a differentiated value proposition based on competitive insights and assess core capabilities that drive advantage.

- **Connect:** Establish management systems to track progress and adapt strategies using real-time feedback from customers and collaborators.
- **Develop Strategy:** Ensure the "Playing to Win" framework's pillars interact effectively, refining strategies based on collaborators and competitors.
- **Implement Strategy:** Create an agile, responsive approach to adapt to changes in customer needs and market dynamics for long-term success.

Mintzberg's 5 Ps of Strategy

Brief History

Henry Mintzberg introduced the 5 Ps of Strategy—Plan, Ploy, Pattern, Position, and Perspective—as a framework for understanding and formulating strategies in his work *The Strategy Concept I: Five Ps for Strategy*.[55] This model offers a more flexible alternative to traditional linear strategic planning, emphasizing a multidimensional approach incorporating adaptability to changing environments.

Model 46 of 50: 5 Ps of Strategy

Mintzberg's 5Ps of Strategy

Plan	Ploy	Pattern	Position	Perspective
Future Orientation	Competitive Disruption	Consistency in Action	Market Positioning	Organizational Culture
Goal Orientation	Unexpected Moves	Emergent Strategy	Differentiation	Strategic Vision
Resources	Deceptive Moves	Learn and Adapt	Value Proposition	Broader Fit (mindset & identity)
Decisions	Diversion Moves			
Risks				

When to Use—Integrating Your 5 Cs Toward a Flexible Strategy

Mintzberg's 5 Ps of Strategy are useful when seeking a dynamic perspective on strategy development. This model is particularly useful when recognizing that strategy is a blend of deliberate planning, competitive tactics, historical behavior, market positioning, and organizational culture. Apply the 5 Ps framework when analyzing strategies to go beyond just deliberate plans (Plan) and consider competitive tactics (Ploy), historical patterns (Pattern), market positioning (Position), and organizational culture (Perspective). This approach is valuable as you aggregate your 5 Cs into a strategic direction.

How to Use

Applying Mintzberg's 5 Ps framework to strategic planning can strengthen your approach to product positioning, customer segmentation, competitive advantage, market climate, and resource allocation. Here is how each "P" can be practically applied:

1. **Plan**
   - **Goal Orientation:** Define objectives around product positioning and customer segmentation. For example, set clear goals on how to position a product in a high-growth segment.
   - **Future Oriented:** Use market forecasts and customer trends to develop plans that leverage competitive resources for a sustainable advantage.
   - **Resource Allocation:** Allocate resources strategically to optimize product development, customer engagement, and distribution based on customer needs and competitor actions.
   - **Decision Framework:** Create guidelines that ensure every decision aligns with maintaining a competitive edge in targeted segments.
   - **Risk Mitigation:** Anticipate risks tied to shifting market climates or competitor moves, preparing contingency plans for product differentiation.
2. **Ploy**
   - **Competitor Disruption:** Identify weaknesses in competitors' product positioning or customer segments and create strategies to capitalize on those, such as launching a product in an underserved market.
   - **Strategic Surprise:** Use unexpected moves—such as entering a new customer segment or offering an innovative feature—to gain a competitive advantage.

- **Psychological Maneuvering**: Leverage tactics that make competitors rethink their strategy, for example, signaling a major product release to deter their market efforts.
- **Deception**: Use controlled misinformation about your product development to divert competitor focus from the real strategic intent.
- **Diversion**: Distract competitors by emphasizing less critical areas of your strategy, allowing you to strengthen more valuable market positions.

3. **Pattern**

- **Consistency in Actions**: Align product offerings and customer engagement in a way that reflects a clear, consistent strategy over time, helping customers recognize and trust the brand.
- **Emergent Strategy:** Pay attention to organic shifts in product demand or customer preferences. For instance, a pattern of customers using your product in a new way could reveal untapped segments.
- **Learning and Adaptation:** Adapt strategies based on past successes or failures in customer targeting and market positioning. Identify patterns that indicate what works in real-world competitive environments.
- **Implicit Strategy:** Maintain a consistent internal strategy for responding to market changes, even if it's not always explicitly articulated. For example, a reliable approach to pricing or product innovation may become part of your competitive identity.

4. **Position**

- **Market Positioning:** Define how your product stands in relation to competitors in terms of price, quality, and innovation. Position it where a customer needs to meet your strengths.
- **Differentiation**: Choose aspects of the product that clearly set it apart from the competition—whether through quality, features, or customer experience—targeting specific customer segments.
- **Value Proposition:** Ensure your product's unique selling points align with customer demands and are communicated clearly to strengthen the competitive position.

- **Environmental Fit:** Align your strengths—such as innovative capabilities or supply chain efficiencies—with current market opportunities and the external business climate.
- **Sustainable Advantage**: Create a position in the market that is hard for competitors to copy, such as through strong brand loyalty or technological leadership.

5. **Perspective**
   - **Organizational Culture**: Your company's values, such as innovation or customer service excellence, should guide product positioning and customer engagement. These values should be reflected in your strategy.
   - **Worldview:** Your strategy should reflect a coherent belief system, such as prioritizing sustainability or customer-centricity. Ensure these perspectives influence your competitive approach.
   - **Strategic Vision**: Align your long-term goals—such as market leadership in a particular segment—with the company's worldview, shaping decisions around resources and competition.
   - **Mindset:** Embrace a growth or innovation mindset that drives strategy evolution, particularly as customer needs and market conditions change.
   - **Identity:** Develop a strong brand identity through strategic decisions, reinforcing how you want to be perceived in relation to competitors and within target customer segments.

By integrating the 5 Ps into strategic planning, businesses can create a holistic approach to navigating competitive landscapes, ensuring product-market fit, targeting key customer segments, and leveraging internal resources for sustained success.

Notes for Your Use

Consider flexibility in the following:

- **Plan:** Define product positioning and customer segmentation goals, using market forecasts to allocate resources effectively and create guidelines for decision making while anticipating risks.

- **Ploy:** Disrupt competitors by identifying their weaknesses, employing strategic surprises, psychological tactics, controlled misinformation, and diversions to strengthen market positions.
- **Pattern:** Maintain consistency in actions, adapt strategies based on customer demand, learn from past experiences, and develop implicit strategies that enhance competitive identity.
- **Position:** Define market position through differentiation, align value propositions with customer demands, and create a sustainable advantage that is hard to replicate.
- **Perspective:** To enhance competitive positioning, shape strategies based on organizational culture and values, ensure alignment with long-term goals, embrace an innovation mindset, and develop a strong brand identity.

Ohmae's 3 Cs Model

Brief History

Kenicki Ohmae introduced the 3 C model in his 1982 book *The Mind of the Strategist: The Art of Japanese Business.*[56] The model integrates three critical elements, the 3 Cs, on which he argues that any effective business strategy should be based: the customer's needs, the corporation's strengths, and the products and services offered by competitors. This model is expanded upon within this book to create the 6 C's.

Model 47 of 50: 3 Cs Model

Ohmae's 3Cs model

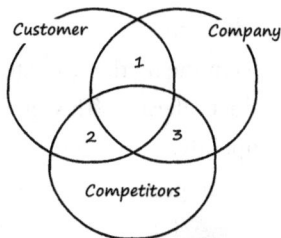

Customer = STP, Value Proposition, etc.
1. Alignment of Company Comp. Advantages
2. Understanding of Competitive moves

Company = Competitive Advantage
3. Understanding of VRIO and declining advantages

When to Use—Integrating Your 5 Cs Toward a Comprehensive Strategy

Use Ohmae's 3 Cs Model when developing your business's strategy. This ensures a holistic approach that integrates organizational strengths, customer needs, and competitive positioning. It's valuable for comprehensive strategic thinking, guiding the alignment of corporate-focused, customer-based, and competitor-based strategies to address key issues and enhance overall strategic effectiveness.

How to Use

Ohmae's 3 C Model—Customer, Company, Competitor—provides a strategic framework for aligning product positioning, customer segmentation, competitive advantage, market climate, and company resources. Here's how to apply each "C" and understand their overlaps:

1. **Customer Strategies**
   - **Segmenting by Objectives**: Identify customer needs through market research, then tailor product positioning and marketing to meet those needs. For example, a segment valuing sustainability should see products emphasizing eco-friendly features, helping create a competitive advantage through differentiation.
   - **Segmenting by Coverage**: Map target markets and match segmentation to customer preferences, adjusting your product's position accordingly. Localized engagement strategies enhance connection, making your brand more competitive by appealing directly to customer segments' specific preferences.
   - **Resegmenting**: Continuously analyze market shifts and customer feedback to identify new segments. This allows timely product innovations, ensuring you stay ahead in competitive markets by meeting emerging needs first.
   - **Adapting to Changes**: Track shifts in the market climate and quickly realign resources and product offerings. This agility allows a business to maintain competitive positioning and customer satisfaction, especially when competitors are slower to respond.

Overlap with Company: Customer insights directly influence product development and marketing, ensuring the company's resources and competencies align with customer needs.

Overlap with Competitor: Monitoring competitors allows you to refine customer segmentation and recognize underserved markets where your company can position itself more advantageously.

2. **Corporate Strategies**
   - **Selectivity and Sequencing**: Focus on core competencies, such as innovation or operational excellence, to create products that outperform competitors. Prioritize growth areas with the highest return on investment and allocate resources accordingly to strengthen competitive positioning.
   - **Make or Buy Decisions**: Evaluate whether to develop new products in-house or outsource based on internal capabilities and competitive pressures. A company with strong R&D might build in-house, while others may outsource to gain a competitive edge without heavy investment in new resources.
   - **Cost-Effectiveness**: Conduct a cost–benefit analysis to streamline operations and reduce costs, ensuring competitive pricing without sacrificing quality. Focus on high-margin products and leverage economies of scale to optimize resource use, reinforcing a sustainable competitive advantage.

   Overlap with Customer: The company's focus on core competencies must align with customer needs, whether they are innovation, affordability, or premium quality. This creates customer loyalty and positions the company as a market leader in its chosen segment.

   Overlap with Competitor: Understanding competitor cost structures and profit margins helps identify where your company can improve efficiency or offer better value, ensuring your corporate strategy strengthens your competitive positioning.

3. **Competitor Strategies**
   - **Power of Image**: Brand positioning is crucial in differentiating your company's products from competitors. Storytelling and strong brand identity create an emotional connection with customers, enhancing competitive advantage. Consistently monitor competitor messaging to ensure your brand remains distinctive.

- **Profit and Cost-Structure Differences**: Analyze competitors' pricing and cost structures to uncover opportunities to offer better value. This might involve adjusting your pricing strategy or enhancing product features, making your offering more attractive to price-sensitive segments.
- **"Hito-Kane-Mono"**: (People, Money, Things) Ensure efficient resource allocation by streamlining processes. Utilize human, financial, and physical resources to support strategic objectives, allowing you to outcompete rivals through superior execution and operational efficiency.

Overlap with Customer: Competitive intelligence helps you adjust customer strategies, such as offering additional value in pricing or features and ensuring customer satisfaction and loyalty.

Overlap with Company: Competitor strategies push the company to optimize resource use and refine internal processes, ensuring that your business remains competitive and agile in responding to market changes.

4. **Overlap Applications**
   - **Customer/Company Overlap**: Use customer feedback to directly inform product development and marketing strategies. This ensures that the company's strengths are aligned with customer needs, enhancing loyalty. For example, if customers favor customization, the company can leverage its production capabilities to offer personalized products.
   - **Customer/Company/Competitor Overlap**: Differentiation is critical in competitive markets where direct price competition is risky. Focus on creating a unique value proposition and communicating it effectively to customers, ensuring they perceive the value and remain loyal, even in the face of cheaper alternatives.
   - **Customer/Competitor Overlap**: Regularly monitor competitors' actions and shifts in customer preferences. If a competitor's new product gains traction, quickly adapt your product features or marketing approach to recapture attention. This rapid response ensures you stay competitive in fast-changing markets.
   - **Competition/Company Overlap**: Competitive intelligence helps companies anticipate competitor moves, such as pricing changes

or new product launches. Ethical considerations are crucial to avoid practices like price fixing or collusion. Maintaining fair competition ensures long-term sustainability and market trust.

By applying Ohmae's 3 Cs Model, you can align your strategies with customer needs, optimize their internal resources, and maintain a competitive edge. The overlap among the three "Cs" highlights the interdependence of understanding customer behavior, leveraging corporate strengths, and positioning against competitors. This holistic approach allows you to create a well-rounded strategy that adapts to market changes and sustains competitive advantage.

Notes for Your Use

- **Gather Information:** Identify customer needs through market research; segment by objectives and coverage; monitor competitor actions and market shifts.
- **Evaluate:** Analyze market conditions and competitor strategies to inform product positioning, corporate strengths, and customer preferences.
- **Connect:** Align customer insights with company capabilities, ensuring product development and marketing resonate with target segments.
- **Develop Strategy:** Focus on core competencies and create a strong brand identity, differentiating products while optimizing resource allocation for competitive advantage.
- **Implement Strategy:** Execute plans with agility, continuously adapting to market changes and competitor actions to maintain customer satisfaction and loyalty.

Porter's Generic Strategies

Brief History

In his 1985 book *Competitive Advantage: Creating and Sustaining Superior Performance*, Michael Porter introduced three core strategies for achieving competitive advantage: cost leadership, differentiation, and focus.[57]

He divided the focus strategy into two types—cost focus and differentiation focus. Porter's framework emphasizes the importance of understanding industry attractiveness and strategically positioning a company to achieve and maintain a competitive edge.

Model 48 of 50: Porter's Generic Strategies

Porter's Generic Strategies

Differentiation	Cost Leadership	Focus Differentiation	Focus Cost
Offer unique products or services that provide added value	Become the lowest-cost producer in the industry	Captures unique product or service advantage	Capture cost advantage within a niche
Capture scope in the market using product and geography advantage	Capture scale in the market using competitive cost advantage	Scope in a narrow market	Scale in a narrow market
Broad Industry Level		Narrow, Product, or Market Level	

When to Use—Compiling Your 5 Cs to Select Your ONE Strategy

Use Porter's Generic Strategies to align your organization in a clear direction for competitive advantage. These strategies, which encompass cost leadership, differentiation, or niche focus, guide decision making to achieve a sustainable edge in the market. By aligning your prior 5 Cs analysis with one of these fundamental approaches, you can effectively tailor your tactics, resources, and positioning to outperform competitors and thrive in their chosen market segments.

How to Use

Porter's Generic Strategies offer practical paths for you to achieve competitive advantage by focusing on cost leadership, differentiation, or a focus strategy. Each of these can be applied strategically to product positioning, customer segmentation, competitive advantage, market climate, and company resources. Here's how to apply each in detail:

1. **Differentiation Strategy**
   - **Objective**: Differentiate by offering unique products or services that stand out in the market.

- **Approach**: Companies pursuing differentiation should focus on delivering unique features, superior quality, exceptional customer service, or advanced technology. Product positioning becomes key: the product must be positioned as a premium offering that justifies a higher price, appealing to customers who value these features.
- **Customer Segmentation**: Differentiation targets customer segments that are willing to pay more for exclusivity, innovation, or added value. These customers typically seek quality and are less price-sensitive.
- **Competitive Advantage**: By offering something competitors cannot easily replicate, such as cutting-edge technology or superior service, the company can build strong brand loyalty and customer retention.
- **Market Climate**: Differentiation is most effective in markets where consumers value variety and innovation or where technological advancements quickly become obsolete.
- **Company Resources**: Successful differentiation relies on unique resources such as R&D capabilities, brand strength, and skilled personnel. Heavy investment in innovation, marketing, and customer experience is necessary to maintain this edge.

2. **Cost Leadership Strategy**
   - **Objective**: Become the lowest-cost producer in the industry while maintaining acceptable quality.
   - **Approach**: Companies should focus on driving down production and operational costs through efficient processes, economies of scale, and cost-cutting innovations. Product positioning centers on affordability, ensuring products are priced lower than competitors without sacrificing quality.
   - **Customer Segmentation**: This strategy targets price-sensitive customer segments who prioritize cost over brand or features. These consumers seek functional products at the best possible price.
   - **Competitive Advantage**: Cost leadership allows a company to offer lower-priced products while still maintaining profitability, undercutting competitors who cannot match the efficiency. This can lead to capturing a larger market share.

- ○ **Market Climate**: This strategy thrives in competitive markets with commoditized products, where customers are driven by price. However, cost leadership also requires staying alert to changes in input costs or competitor price wars.
- ○ **Company Resources**: Effective cost leadership depends on large-scale production capabilities, efficient supply chain management, and tight cost controls. The company's ability to innovate in cost reduction is a critical resource.

3. **Focus Strategy**
   - ○ **Objective**: Focus on a narrow market segment—whether defined by geography, customer type, or product line—and tailor offerings to meet its specific needs.
   - ○ **Approach**: Companies pursuing a focus strategy can use either differentiation or cost leadership within their niche market. This involves deep understanding of the target segment and customizing products or services specifically for them.
   - ○ **Customer Segmentation**: Focus strategy targets niche markets with unique needs, where broader competitors either overlook the segment or fail to serve it well. For example, a luxury brand may focus exclusively on high-net-worth individuals.
   - ○ **Competitive Advantage**: By concentrating resources on a particular segment, a company can build specialized expertise, customer loyalty, and a strong competitive position in that niche. It often faces fewer direct competitors within the segment.
   - ○ **Market Climate**: Focus strategies are effective in markets with clear, underserved segments with specific needs. These could be fragmented markets or markets where customer preferences vary widely.
   - ○ **Company Resources**: Success in focus strategies requires an intimate knowledge of the target market and the ability to customize offerings to its needs. Resources are concentrated on perfecting the product or service for that segment, whether through product development or highly targeted marketing.

4. **Stuck in the Middle**
   - ○ **Situation**: A company is "stuck in the middle" if it tries to combine differentiation and cost leadership without fully committing to either.

- ○ **Consequence**: Without a clear competitive advantage, the company risks losing market share to low-cost providers and premium, differentiated competitors. The firm's resources are spread too thin, lacking a strong identity.
- ○ **Exceptions**: A company may still survive in a highly attractive industry with little competition or if all competitors are similarly "stuck in the middle." However, this is rare and generally unsustainable over the long term.

Each strategy relies on a clear understanding of customer segmentation, product positioning, and how to leverage company resources to maintain competitive advantage. Trying to pursue multiple strategies simultaneously, however, risks losing a distinct edge, leading to a "stuck in the middle" scenario where competitive advantage is diluted. Successful firms choose a clear strategic path aligned with their core strengths and market conditions.

Notes for Your Use

- **Gather Information:** Assess market conditions, customer preferences, and the competitive landscape to determine the most suitable strategy for gaining a competitive advantage.
- **Evaluate:** Analyze the potential for differentiation, cost leadership, or focus strategies based on customer segments, resource capabilities, and market climate.
- **Connect:** Align product positioning and customer segmentation with chosen strategies, ensuring they resonate with target audiences and leverage company strengths.
- **Develop Strategy:** Choose one clear path—differentiation through unique offerings, cost leadership for price-sensitive consumers, or focus on niche markets tailored to specific needs.
- **Implement Strategy:** Execute the selected strategy with dedicated resources and continuous monitoring, maintaining a clear competitive identity to avoid a "stuck in the middle" scenario.

Hambrick and Fredrickson's Strategy Diamond

Brief History

Hambrick and Fredrickson introduced the Strategy Diamond in their 2001 article "Are You Sure You Have a Strategy?"[58] The strategy diamond framework presents five interrelated elements—arenas, differentiators, vehicles, staging, and economic logic—that help organizations craft comprehensive and coherent strategies. The Strategy Diamond emphasizes the need to align these elements to achieve a sustainable competitive advantage.

Model 49 of 50: Strategy Diamond

Hambrick and Fredrickson's Strategy Diamond

Arenas	Vehicles	Differentiators	Staging & Pacing	Economic
Markets & Customer Segments	Methods of Competing Collaborators	Unique Value Proposition and Competitive Advantages	Timing and Sequence of Initiatives	Value Generation

When to Use—Integrating Your 5 Cs into an Aligned Strategy with Competitive Advantage

Use the Strategy Diamond when you need a concise and visual way to depict and understand the interconnected components of a business strategy. Use your prior work on the 5 Cs to better understand how arenas, differentiators, economic logic, vehicles, and staging and pacing collectively shape your business's strategic direction.

How to Use

Hambrick and Fredrickson's Strategy Diamond provides a structured framework for organizations to develop and implement effective strategies by linking key components.

1. **Arenas = Customers**
   - **Application**: Identify and define the specific markets and customer segments the organization will target.

- ○ **Product Positioning**: Clearly outline where the product fits within the market landscape. For instance, if targeting the luxury segment, the positioning should emphasize exclusivity and high quality.
- ○ **Customer Segmentation**: Segment the market based on demographics, psychographics, and behavior to tailor offerings. Understanding the unique needs of different segments will inform product development and marketing strategies.
- ○ **Competitive Advantage**: Knowing which arenas to compete in helps the company establish a competitive advantage by focusing resources on areas with high potential for success.
- ○ **Market Climate**: Evaluate current market trends, competitive dynamics, and potential growth opportunities in identified arenas to ensure alignment with organizational goals.
- ○ **Company Resources**: Assess the organization's capabilities and resources to determine which arenas are feasible for entry and long-term success.

2. **Vehicles = Characteristics**
- ○ **Application**: Decide the channels and means of competing in the chosen arenas.
- ○ **Product Positioning**: The choice of vehicles—direct sales, online platforms, or retail partnerships—will influence how customers perceive and access the product.
- ○ **Customer Segmentation**: Select vehicles that resonate with the target segments. For example, high-tech products may benefit from online sales and tech partnerships, while consumer goods might be better served through traditional retail.
- ○ **Competitive Advantage**: Choose vehicles that enhance the competitive position, such as exclusive partnerships or proprietary distribution channels that limit competitors' access to the market.
- ○ **Market Climate**: Analyze market conditions to determine the effectiveness of different vehicles. For example, in a rapidly changing tech environment, agility in distribution channels may be crucial.

- ○ **Company Resources**: Leverage existing capabilities and resources when selecting vehicles. For instance, a company with strong logistics capabilities may opt for direct distribution to improve efficiency.

3. **Differentiators = Competitors**
   - ○ **Application**: Identify and enhance the unique value propositions that set the organization apart from competitors.
   - ○ **Product Positioning**: Use differentiators to craft compelling messaging and positioning strategies that resonate with target customers, such as highlighting innovative features, superior quality, or exceptional customer service.
   - ○ **Customer Segmentation**: Tailor differentiators to meet the specific needs and preferences of different customer segments. For example, eco-conscious consumers may value sustainability-focused differentiators.
   - ○ **Competitive Advantage**: Leverage differentiators to build brand loyalty and create barriers to entry for competitors, making it difficult for them to replicate unique offerings.
   - ○ **Market Climate**: Adapt differentiators based on market trends and shifts. For instance, if competitors focus on price, enhancing product features or customer service can provide a competitive edge.
   - ○ **Company Resources**: Ensure that the organization has the necessary resources, such as skilled personnel, technology, and marketing capabilities, to deliver on its differentiators effectively.

4. **Staging and Pacing = Climate**
   - ○ **Application**: Define the timing and sequence of strategic initiatives.
   - ○ **Product Positioning**: Consider the timing of product launches and market entry to maximize impact and relevance.
   - ○ **Customer Segmentation**: Tailor the pacing of initiatives based on the readiness and responsiveness of target segments. Some segments may adopt new products quickly, while others may require more education and engagement.
   - ○ **Competitive Advantage**: Execute strategic initiatives in a way that outpaces competitors, allowing the organization to establish a strong foothold in the market before rivals can react.

- ○ **Market Climate**: Adjust staging based on market conditions, such as economic shifts or competitor actions, ensuring flexibility in the strategic approach.
- ○ **Company Resources**: Align resource allocation with the pacing of initiatives. Ensure that the company has the necessary resources available at each stage to execute effectively without overextending.

5. **Economic Logic = Company**
   - ○ **Application**: Articulate how the strategy will generate profits and create value.
   - ○ **Product Positioning**: Ensure that pricing strategies align with the value proposition and reflect the unique positioning in the market. Higher-priced, differentiated products may require a clear value articulation to justify costs.
   - ○ **Customer Segmentation**: Understand the pricing sensitivity and WTP within different segments, adjusting economic models to capture maximum value.
   - ○ **Competitive Advantage**: Establish clear economic logic differentiating the company from competitors, such as lower costs, superior margins, or unique revenue streams.
   - ○ **Market Climate**: Monitor economic conditions and adjust economic models accordingly to maintain profitability in changing environments.
   - ○ **Company Resources**: Ensure that the economic logic is supported by the company's operational capabilities and resource allocation, optimizing cost structures to sustain profitability.

You can develop a robust strategic framework that aligns with your goals and market conditions by systematically applying each component of Hambrick and Fredrickson's Strategy Diamond. This approach fosters strategic coherence by ensuring that all elements—arenas, vehicles, differentiators, staging and pacing, and economic logic—are interconnected and work harmoniously to achieve competitive advantage. Additionally, by considering product positioning, customer segmentation, and company resources within each element, you can effectively navigate the complexities of their markets and implement successful strategies.

Notes for Your Use

- **Gather Information:** Identify and analyze target markets, customer segments, and competitive landscapes to inform strategic components of the Strategy Diamond.
- **Evaluate:** Assess each component—arenas, vehicles, differentiators, staging and pacing, and economic logic—to ensure alignment with organizational goals and market conditions.
- **Connect:** Link product positioning, customer segmentation, and company resources to the Strategy Diamond components, ensuring coherence across the strategic framework.
- **Develop Strategy:** Formulate a comprehensive strategy by defining specific arenas to compete, selecting appropriate vehicles, enhancing differentiators, planning staging and pacing, and articulating economic logic for profitability.
- **Implement Strategy:** Execute the strategy by focusing on maintaining interconnections among all elements, ensuring resource allocation aligns with initiatives, and adapting to market dynamics for sustained competitive advantage.

The Emergent Approach to Strategy

Brief History

Peter Compo's *Emergent Approach to Strategy* is unique because it is both a theory of strategy (Part I) and a practice (Part II). Both are built on principles from systems thinking, evolutionary biology, and complexity science, moving away from traditional, linear, and cascade-based strategic planning.[59] The essence of the approach is that strategy design and implementation is akin to solving a puzzle as opposed to following sequential steps or filling in canvases, though canvases might be helpful as a supporting technique.

Puzzle solving captures the spirit of the ugly, messy, and sometimes frightening, but exhilarating process of making real change and innovating. By focusing on what's needed to solve the puzzle, and collecting information only when the process demands it, the team can keep its energy through tough times. The puzzle is an alternative to cascades or "plumbing diagrams" that lays out sequential steps.

Rather than a static plan or a collection of choices, Compo advocates for a guiding "central rule" that supports adaptive decision making and addresses bottlenecks hindering progress toward aspirations. His work builds on earlier adaptive strategies and emergent processes from thinkers like Henry Mintzberg, who emphasized the need for flexible, evolving approaches over rigid planning.

Model 50 of 50: The Emergent Strategy Approach

Emergent Strategy Approach

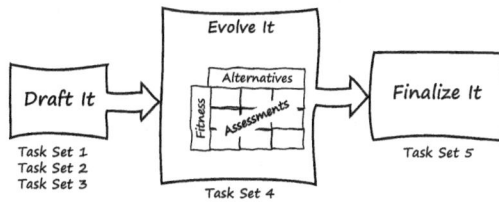

When to Use—Whenever You Need a Strategy and Not a Plan

You need a true strategy when there is uncertainty about the future and when there are multiple functions in the organization that need guidance on actions and decisions. Because the *Emergent Approach* is not based on a specific business model or specific strategy advice, it is much more flexible than other approaches and applies to any situation. It is the aspiration of your endeavor that defines the scope of the work. The approach can apply to an overall business unit or corporation, and it can apply to a function like IT, HR, manufacturing, product development, marketing, or sales. It can apply to a smaller-scope question, such as "How do we simplify the product line?" or "How do we improve quality control?" and it can apply to broad-scope questions like "How do we raise the profitability or sales rate of the company?" or "Should we consider an acquisition?"

The Emergent Approach applies no matter the volatility level and complexity of your situation because scenario planning and exploration of alternatives is inherent in the process, and not "add on" to be considered later.

The approach draws parallels between business strategy and natural evolution, suggesting that effective strategies should continuously adapt, evolve, and respond to changing "fitness landscapes"—environments shaped by competition, regulation, technology, and customer preferences. Sometimes your strategy framework requires significant changes; other times, minor adjustments suffice.

How to Use

Two concepts guide your of the emergent approach: Instead of following sequential steps, the discipline of the design process is based on design principles. And second, focus on diagnosing and "busting" the bottleneck to achieving aspirations—which is the key to identifying the strategy. Here are more details:

- **Strategy Framework Components:** A strategy is the central rule or policy aimed at resolving the bottleneck to achieving aspirations. It provides real-time, unifying guidance for actions and decisions. A strategy is just one, but the most important component of a strategy framework (often called a strategic plan), as shown below. Specifically, it is a central rule or policy designed to "bust" the bottleneck to achieving aspirations. The strategy supplies unifying real-time guidance for taking action and making decisions.

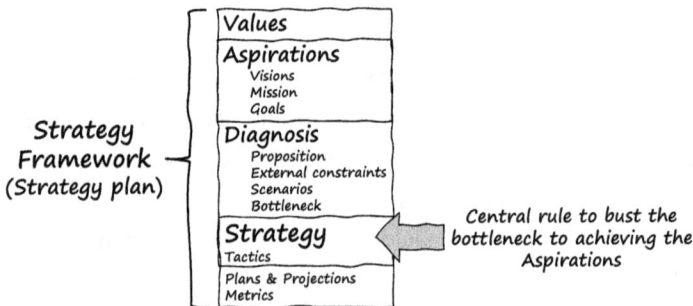

Strategy Framework (Strategy plan)

Values
Aspirations
    Visions
    Mission
    Goals
Diagnosis
    Proposition
    External constraints
    Scenarios
    Bottleneck
Strategy
    Tactics
    Plans & Projections
    Metrics

Central rule to bust the bottleneck to achieving the Aspirations

- **Strategy Alternative Matrix (SAM):** The core tool for designing a strategy framework, adaptable to the scope and complexity of the endeavor. The SAM range from simple to highly detailed depending on the ambition of the aspiration. Use the SAM to organize your team's thoughts.

- The process for creating the SAM is not a cascade, but rather an agile process where you draft a minimum viable SAM, and then evolve it using all the information from all the relevant people. This is the overarching model.

Framework Alternatives

	Alternative 1	Alternative 2	Alternative n
Alternatives Section — Values			
Aspirations Visions Mission Goals			
Diagnosis Proposition External constraints Scenarios Bottleneck			
Strategy Tactics Plans & Projections Metrics			
Fitness Section — Fitness Criteria 1	Assessment	Assessment	Assessment
Fitness Criteria 2	Assessment	Assessment	Assessment
Fitness Criteria n	Assessment	Assessment	Assessment

Fitness Assessment

- **Strategy-Bottleneck-Aspiration Triad:** Simplifies the framework into its three most essential components and acts as a starting point for strategy processes or, in some cases, leads to direct identification of a useful strategy.

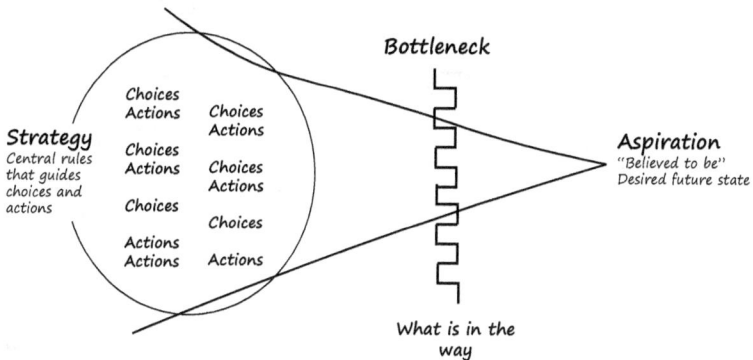

Strategy
Central rules that guides choices and actions

Choices / Actions

Bottleneck

Aspiration
"Believed to be"
Desired future state

What is in the way

- **Adapt with the five Task Sets:** Use the task sets as a flexible guide. These tasks are adaptable, based on design principles that allow the strategy to evolve in stages. Each Task Set includes objectives that vary in complexity and duration, depending on project scope, team skills, and available time.

Task Set 1: Set the Stage & Organize 1a. Articulate Reasons to Reopen the Strategy Process 1b. Sketch Your Nested System 1c. Design Rules and Teams 1d. Capture Initial Ideas 1e. Design a Training Approach 1f. Design Timelines and Milestones 1g. Complete, Name, and Socialize Plan of Attack	**Task Set 3: Draft or Modify Scenarios** 3a. Capture Environmental Conditions & Events 3b. Construct Scenarios 3c. Incorporate Draft Scenarios into Your SAM
	Task Set 4: Evolve the SAM until a Compelling Framework Emerges Task Set 4 is where you will spend the majority of your time. You have drafted your SAM, and now work it until a compelling strategy framework alternative emerges.
Task Set 2: Draft or Modify the Strategy Alternative Matrix (SAM) 2a. Choose Template & Capture Current Framework 2b. Discover & Articulate Values 2c. Draft or Modify Aspirations 2d. Draft or Modify Diagnosis: Proposition, Constraints 2e. Draft or Modify Your Diagnosis: Bottlenecks 2f. Draft or Modify Fitness Criteria 2g. Draft or Modify Alternatives 2h. Add Initial Tactics, Plans, Metrics, or Assessments	**Task Set 5: Transition to Implementation** 5a. Complete Plans, Policies, Budgets, & Organizatioin 5b. Design Four-stations Dashboard and Triggers 5c. Complete Charters and Nested Frameworks 5d. Make Rollout Decisions 5e. Complete working Documents

These task sets are not rigid steps but instead promote an adaptive, experimental mindset—encouraging cycles of diagnosis, design, and implementation as the strategy unfolds. The ultimate goal is to build a flexible "strategy framework" that includes interconnected elements: beliefs, values, aspirations, diagnosis, and strategic principles.

In all cases, treat the design as an ongoing evolution where sometimes you need to make a large change to your strategy framework and other times to make a small one.

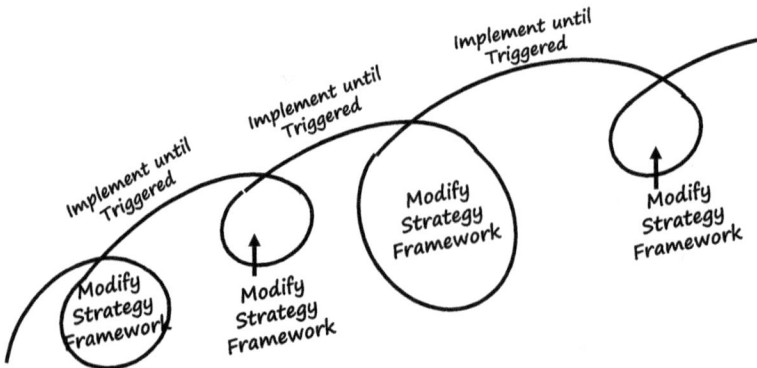

Notes for Your Use

- **Gather Information Only When Needed:** Many strategical processes grind to a halt just because most of the time is spent collecting financial, share, and market data with no questions articulated. Align your 5 Cs on questions or triggers.
- **Use the Four-Station Dashboard:** Identify triggers for modifying your strategy framework.
- **Use the Five Disqualifiers:** Test your strategy component and other components of this framework as you go. The five disqualifiers are a new, more adaptive, set of tests of strategy: emergentapproach.com/disqualifiers/
- **Use Scenarios in More Advanced Endeavors:** shows the techniques for making scenarios practical.
- **When Stuck, Go Back to the Simple Triad and Focus on the Bottleneck:** Correctly identifying the bottleneck to achieving your aspiration is the key to finding strategy. A problem well-articulated is half solved!

Concluding Thoughts

As you conclude this journey through the *Strategy Toolbox*, I hope the models and frameworks have offered a clear pathway to translate information into impactful strategies. At the heart of this book, the **5 Is model**—Information, Issues, Insights, Implications, and Implementation—served as a reminder that true strategic advantage emerges from more than just data gathering. By guiding you from raw information through critical insights to actionable implications, this model encouraged a structured yet adaptable approach, turning complexity into clarity. Through the 5 Is, you practiced shifting from analysis to action, honing the ability to craft strategies that drive accurate, implementable results. Along the way, you should have continued to engage your team in dialogue around the analysis. Hopefully, the tools helped you AND your team organize the discussions.

Alongside the 5 Is, the **6 Cs framework**—Company, Characteristics, Customers, Competitors, Climate, and Consolidation—provided a structured lens for analyzing different facets of the business environment. Moving from internal strengths to uncontrollable external forces, each section illustrated how diverse models could apply to specific strategic questions, leading you from situational analysis to cohesive planning. This structure reinforced the idea that strategic insights arise when models are contextualized thoughtfully and integrated into the broader organizational landscape though active discussion with your team.

As you continue to apply these models, remember that this book aimed to bridge theory and practice, equipping you and your team with tools that can adapt across settings. I hope you feel empowered not only to understand these models but to use them dynamically—to test, adapt, and refine them within the realities of your own strategic challenges.

In parting, may the lessons here serve as more than just a reference, becoming catalysts for ongoing discussions, thoughtful analysis, and impactful implementation. Let these models inspire you to move confidently from insight to implementation, converting ideas into strategic actions that shape meaningful outcomes and create sustained, impactful success.

About the Author

Simon Reese is an award-winning management professor and corporate strategist with a Fortune 500 company. With a wealth of experience exceeding two decades, Dr. Reese has been at the forefront of guiding businesses and sculpting innovative strategies for market entry, expansion, and strategic exits. He has also contributed extensively to scholarly literature, with over thirty publications covering diverse topics from strategy to organizational learning and business agility. He holds lecturer and adjunct professor positions at Rice University, Jones School of Business; Northeastern University, College of Professional Studies; and University of Maryland, Global Campus. Through these roles, he has reached thousands of students, bridging theory and practice by teaching models that clarify, organize, and develop implementable strategies. He is also a former associate editor of *The Learning Organization*, a journal dedicated to exploring the dynamics of collective learning and collaborative growth within organizations.

Endnotes

1. E. Penrose, *The Theory of the Growth of the Firm* (Oxford University Press, 1959).
2. B. Wernerfelt, "A Resource-Based View of a Firm," *Strategic Management Journal* 5, no. 2 (1984): 171–80, https://doi.org/10.1002/smj.4250050207.
3. J. Barney, "Firm Resources and Sustained Competitive," *Journal of Management*, 17, no. 1 (1991): 99–120, https://doi.org/10.1177/014920639101700108.
4. M. E. Porter, *Competitive Advantage: Creating and Sustaining Superior Performance* (Free Press, 1985).
5. J. Magretta, *Understanding Michael Porter: The Essential Guide to Competition and Strategy* (Harvard Business Press, 2012).
6. Barney, Firm Resources and Sustained Competitive," 99–120.
7. J. A. Kay, *Foundations of Corporate Success : How Business Strategies Add Value* (Oxford University Press, 1995).
8. J. Kay, "The Structure of Strategy," *Business Strategy Review* 4, no. 2 (1993): 17–37, https://doi.org/10.1111/j.1467-8616.1993.tb00049.x.
9. R. F. Stewart, O. J. Benepe, and A. Mitchell, *Formal Planning: the Staff Planner's Role at Startup (No. 250)* (Stanford Research Institute, 1965).
10. R. Puyt, F. B. Lie, F. De Graaf, and C. P. M. Wilderom, "Origins of SWOT Analysis," *Academy of Management Proceedings* 2020, no. 1 (2020), https://doi.org/10.5465/AMBPP.2020.132.
11. R. Puyt, F. Lie, and C, P. M. Wilderom, "The Origins of SWOT Analysis," *Long Range Planning* 56, no. 3 (2023): 1–24, https://www.sciencedirect.com/science/article/pii/S0024630123000110.
12. H. Weihrich, "The TOWS Matrix—A Tool for Situational Analysis," *Long Range Planning* 15, no. 2 (1982): 54–66.
13. J. Stavros, "From Foundation to Flight: SOAR's Journey from Appreciative Inquiry to AI Practitioner," *AI Practitioner: International Journal of Appreciative Inquiry* 26, no. 2 (2024): 13–25.
14. J. Stavros, D. L. Cooperrider, and L. Kelley, "Strategic Inquiry with Appreciative Intent: Inspiration to SOARAI Practitioner," *International Journal of Appreciative Inquiry* 5, no. 4 (2003): 10–17.
15. J. Stavros and G. Hinrichs, *Learning to SOAR: Creating Strategy that Invites Inspiration and Innovation* (SOAR Institute, 2021).
16. P. Kotler, *Marketing Management: Analysis, Planning, Implementation, and Control*, 8th ed. (Prentice Hall, 1994).

17. P. Kotler and Sidney J. Levy, "Broadening the Concept of Marketing," *Journal of Marketing* 33, no. 1 (1969): 10–15.

18. E. M. Rogers, *Diffusion of Innovations* (The Free Press of Glencoe, 1962), 367 pp.

19. E. M. Rogers, *Diffusion of Innovations*, 5th ed. (The Free Press of Glencoe, 2003), 550 pp.

20. R. Vernon, "International Investment and International Trade in the Product Cycle," *Quarterly Journal of Economics* 80, no. 2 (1966): 190–207. https://doi.org/10.2307/1880689.

21. R. Manes, "A New Dimension to Breakeven Analysis," *Journal of Accounting Research* 4, no. 1 (1966): 87–100, https://doi.org/10.2307/2490143.

22. B. Henderson, "The Product Portfolio," *BCG*, January 1, 1970, https://www.bcg.com/publications/1970/strategy-the-product-portfolio.

23. M. Baghai, C. Coley, and D. David White, *The Alchemy of Growth: Practical Insights for Building the Enduring Enterprise* (Perseus Publishing, 1999).

24. C. M. Christensen and M. E. Raynor, *The Innovator's Solution: Creating and Sustaining Successful Growth* (Harvard Business Review Press, 2003).

25. C. M. Christensen, R. G. McGrath, and M. E. Raynor, *Competing Against Luck: The Story of Innovation and Customer Choice* (HarperBusiness, 2016).

26. A. Ulwick, *What Customers Want: Using Outcome-Driven Innovation to Create Breakthrough Products and Services* (McGraw-Hill, 2005), 202 pp.

27. Abraham H. Maslow, "A Theory of Human Motivation," *Psychological Review* 50, no. 4 (1943): 370–96.

28. E. Almquist, J. Senior, and N. Block, "The Elements of Value: Measuring and Delivering What Customers Really Want," *Harvard Business Review*, September, 2018, https://hbr.org/2016/09/the-elements-of-value.

29. E. Almquist, J. Cleghorn, and L. Sherer, "The B2B Elements of Value," *Harvard Business Review* March–April, 2018, https://hbr.org/2018/03/the-b2b-elements-of-value.

30. A. Osterwalder, Y. Pigneur, G. Bernarda, and A. Smith, *Value Proposition Design: How to Create Products and Services Customer Want* (John Wiley & Sons, 2014).

31. S. Reese, "Inter-Company Interaction Framework: Understanding the 4 Cs Framework to Promote Learning," *Industrial and Commercial Training* 47, no. 2 (2015): 67–72, https://doi.org/10.1108/ICT-10-2014-0066.

32. W. R. Smith, "Product Differentiation and Market Segmentation as Alternative Marketing Strategies," *Journal of Marketing* 21, no. 1 (1956): 3–8.

33. A. Ries and J. Trout, "The Positioning Era Cometh," *Advertising Age* 24, no. 1 (1972): 35–38.

34. A. Ries and J. Trout, *Positioning: The Battle for Your Mind* (McGraw-Hill, 1981).

35. F. Oberholzer-Gee, *Better, Simpler Strategy: A Value-Based Guide to Exceptional Performance* (Harvard Business Review Press, 2021).

36. A. Hirschman, *National Power and the Structure of Foreign Trade* (University of California Press, 1945).

37. B. Henderson, "The Rule of Three and Four," *BCG*, January 1, 1976, https://www.bcg.com/publications/1976/business-unit-strategy-growth-rule-three-four.

38. M. Reeves, M. Deimler, G. Stalk, and F. Scognamiglio, "BCG Classics Revisited: The Rule of Three and Four," *BCG*, December 4, 2012. https://www.bcg.com/publications/2012/business-unit-strategy-the-rule-of-three-and-four-bcg-classics-revisited.

39. M. E. Porter, *Competitive Strategy: Techniques for Analyzing Industries and Competitors* (Free Press, 1980).

40. M. S. Hunt, "Competition in the Major Home Appliance Industry 1960–1970" (Unpublished Doctoral diss., Harvard University, 1972).

41. Porter, *Competitive Strategy.*

42. J. C. Short, D. J. Ketchen, T. Palmer, and G. T. Hult, "Firm, Strategic Group, and Industry Influences on Performance," *Strategic Management Journal* 28, no. 2 (2007): 147–67, https://doi.org/10.1002/smj.574.

43. L. Van Valen, "A New Evolutionary Law," *Evolutionary Theory* 1: 1–30.

44. S. C. Voelpel, M. Leibold, E. B. Tekie, and G. von Krogh, "Escaping the Red Queen Effect in Competitive Strategy," *European Management Journal* 23, no. 1 (2005): 37–49, https://doi.org/10.1016/j.emj.2004.12.008.

45. A. M. Brandenburger and B. J. Nalebuff, *Co-Opetition* (Currency Doubleday, 1996).

46. P. Ghemawat, "Distance Still Matters: The Hard Reality of Global Expansion," *Harvard Business Review* 79, no. 8 (2001): 137–47.

47. F. J. Aguilar, *Scanning the Business Environment* (Macmillan, 1967).

48. M. E. Porter, *The Competitive Advantage of Nations* (Free Press, 1990).

49. Porter, *Competitive Strategy.*

50. O. Gadiesh and J. L. Gilbert, "Profit Pools: A Fresh Look at Strategy," *Harvard Business Review* 76, no. 3 (1998): 139–47.

51. Vernon, "International Investment and International Trade in the Product Cycle," 190–207.

52. A. J. Rowe, R. O. Mason, K. E. Dickel, R. B. Mann, and R. J. Mockler *Strategic Management: A Methodological Approach* (Addison-Wesley, 1974).

53. J. A. Vasconcellos e Sá, *Strategy Moves: 14 Complete Attack and Defense Strategies for Competitive Advantage* (Prentice-Hall Financial Times, 2005).

54. A. G. Lafley and R. Martin *Playing to Win: How Strategy Really Works* (Harvard Business Review Press, 2013).

55. H. Mintzberg, "The Strategy Concept I: Five Ps for Strategy," *California Management Review* 30, no. 1 (1987): 11–24.

56. K. Ohmae, *The Mind of the Strategist: The Art of Japanese Business* (McGraw-Hill, 1982).

57. Porter, *Competitive Advantage.*

58. D. C. Hambrick and J. W. Fredrickson, "Are You Sure You Have a Strategy?," *Academy of Management Perspectives* 15, no. 4 (2001): 48–59, https://doi.org/10.5465/ame.2001.5897655.

59. P. Compo, *The Emergent Approach to Strategy: Adaptive Design and Execution* (Business Expert Press, 2022).

Index

A

Added value, 127
ADL Matrix, 158–162
  actions across industry life
    cycle, 158
  brief history, 158
  context and scenarios of use,
    158–160
  how to use, 160–162
Aggressive strategy, 169–170
Aguilar, Francis, 137
Almquist, Eric, 67
Attack and Defense Strategy plan,
    173–179
  attack strategies, 177
  brief history, 173–174
  defense strategies, 178–179
  develop your strategic plan, 174
  how to use, 174–177
Augmented level products, 36
Automotive industry, 81

B

Barney, Jay, 11
Benchmarking and best practices, 142
Bernarda, Gregory, 71
Beverage company, 82
Bloch, Nicolas, 67
Blocking entry, 178
Boston Consulting Group (BCG)
    Growth-Share Matrix,
    52–56
  brief history, 52
  business units, 52–53
  context and scenario to use,
    53–54
  how to use, 54–55
Brand management, 34
Brandenburger, Adam M., 124
Break down costs to serve, 91

Break-Even Analysis, 45–48
  brief history, 45
  context and scenario to use,
    46–47
  key sensitivities, 46
  how to use, 47–48
Break-Even Point, 47–48
Broadening the Concept of
    Marketing, 33
Business goal alignment, 176
Business-to-business (B2B), 67
Business-to-consumer (B2C), 66

C

CAC. *See* Customer Acquisition
    Cost (CAC)
CAGE analysis, 132–137
  brief history, 132–133
  context and scenarios of use,
    133–134
  host and home country
    distances, 133
  how to use, 134–137
Carroll, Lewis, 120
Christensen, Clayton, 63
Climate
  ADL Matrix, 158–162
  CAGE analysis, 132–137
  climate checklist, 162–163
  Industry Life Cycle Stages,
    152–157
  Industry Profit Pools,
    149–152
  Industry Value Chain Analysis,
    149–152
  inferential and uncontrollable,
    131–132
  PESTEL, 137–140
  Porter's Diamond of National
    Advantage, 140–144
  Porter's Five Forces, 144–149

CLV. *See* Customer Lifetime Value (CLV)
Co-opetition, 124–129
  brief history, 124–125
  competitive partnering, 125
  context and scenario to use, 125–127
  how to use, 127–129
Comparative advantage analysis, 142
Competitive benchmarking, 117
Competitive strategy, 172–173
Competitor analysis, 175
Competitor Profile Matrix, 111–115
  brief history, 111–112
  context and scenario to use, 112–113
  landscape comparison, 112
  how to use, 114–115
Competitors
  Co-opetition, 124–129
  Competitor Checklist, 129–130
  Competitor Profile Matrix, 111–115
  Herfindahl–Hirschman Index (HHI), 99–102
  inferential with almost no control, 97–98
  Porter's Four Corners, 106–111
  Red Queen Effect, 120–124
  Rule of Three and Four, 103–106
  Strategic Group Analysis, 115–120
Conservative strategy, 170–171
Consolidation phase
  3 Cs Model, 187–191
  5-Step Strategy Model, 179–183
  Attack and Defense Strategy plan, 173–179
  cohesive strategic direction, 165–168
  Emergent Approach to Strategy, 200–205
  Generic Strategies, 191–195
  Ps of Strategy, 183–187
  SPACE Analysis, 168–173
  Strategy Diamond, 196–200
Consumer electronics company, 81
Core-level products, 35
Counter-attack, 178

CRM. *See* Customer relationship management (CRM) systems
Cross-selling, 86
Customer Acquisition Cost (CAC), 87
Customer lifespan estimation, 87
Customer Lifetime Value (CLV), 84–88
  brief history, 84
  context and scenario to use, 85–86
  how to use, 86–88
  value of your customers, 84–85
Customer relationship management (CRM) systems, 82
Customer retention, 85
Customer Retention cost, 87
Customer segmentation, 34
Customer segments, 86
Customers and collaborators
  4 Cs of Inter-company Collaboration, 75–79
  customer and collaborator checklist, 94–95
  Customer Lifetime Value (CLV), 84–88
  Hierarchy of Needs, 66–70
  inferential knowledge with less control, 61–62
  Jobs-To-Be-Done theory, 63–66
  Segment–Target–Position (STP), 80–83
  Value Proposition Canvas, 71–75
  Value Stick, 88–94
Cybersecurity, 122

D

Defensive strategy, 171–172
Diamond of National Advantage, 140–144
  brief history, 140
  competitiveness of industries in specific country, 141
  context and scenarios of use, 141–142
  how to use, 143–144
Differentiated circle, 177

Diffusion of innovation, 37–41
    brief history, 37
    context and scenario to use, 37–39
    customer/product match, 37
    how to use, 39–41
Distinctive Capabilities
        Framework, 16
Dohr, James, 45

E

Economic, Technical, Political, and
        Social factors, 137
Emergent Approach to Strategy,
        200–205
    brief history, 200–202
    how to use, 202–205
Escaping the Red Queen Effect in
        Competitive Strategy, 120
Expected-level products, 35

F

Fashion retailer, 81–82
Financial forecasting, 86
Firm Resources and Sustained
        Competitive Advantage, 3
5-Step Strategy Model, 179–183
    brief history, 179–180
    five crucial steps in, 180
    how to use, 180–182
Five Forces, 144–149
    brief history, 144–145
    context and scenarios of use,
        145–146
    forces within your industry, 145
    how to use, 146–149
Flanking attack, 177
4 Cs of Inter-company Collaboration,
        75–79
    brief history, 75
    collaboration toward shared vision,
        75–76
    context and scenario to use, 76–77
    how to use, 77–79
Four Corners, 106–111
    brief history, 106

    competitor's motivation, 107
    context and scenario to use,
        107–108
    how to use, 108–111
Four Corners Model, 106
Frontal attack, 177

G

Gadiesh, Orit, 149
Generic level products, 35
Generic Strategies, 191–195
    brief history, 191
    ONE strategy, 192
    how to use, 192–195
Ghemawat, Pankaj, 132
Gilbert, James, 149
Global Service, 178
Guerrilla attack, 177

H

Henderson, Bruce, 103
Herfindahl–Hirschman Index (HHI),
        99–102
    brief history, 99–100
    context and scenario to use,
        100–101
    how to use, 101–102
HHI. See Herfindahl–Hirschman
        Index (HHI)
Hierarchy of Needs, 66–70
    brief history, 66–67
    context and scenario to use,
        67–69
    customer's seriatim of needs, 67
    how to use, 69–70
Hirschman, Albert O., 99
Holding the ground, 178
Hospitality industry, 82
Hunt, David, 115

I

Industry analysis, 116–117
Industry analysis, 142

Industry Life Cycle Stages, 152–157
  brief history, 152–153
  context and scenarios of use,
    153–155
  stage and determine actions, 153
  how to use, 155–157
Industry Profit Pools, 149–152
  brief history, 149
  context and scenarios of use,
    150–151
  how to use, 151–152
  value sits within industry, 150
Industry Value Chain Analysis,
    149–152
  brief history, 149
  context and scenarios of use,
    150–151
  how to use, 151–152
  value sits within industry, 150
Intangible resources, 5
Isolation attack, 177

J

Jobs-To-Be-Done theory, 63–66
  brief history, 63
  context and scenario to use, 64–65
  customer's fundamental needs,
    63–64
  how to use, 65–66

K

Kay, John, 15
Kay's distinctive capabilities
    framework
  brief history, 15–16
  context and scenario for use, 16–17
  determine your competitive
    advantage, 16
  how to use, 17–19
Key Performance Indicators
    (KPIs), 29
Kotler, Philip, 33, 80
Kotler's 5 product levels, 33–36
  brief history, 33
  context and scenarios for use,
    34–35

  expand consumer value, 33
  product offering toward greatest
    value, 35–36
KPIs. *See* Key Performance Indicators
    (KPIs)

L

Lafley, A.G., 179
Little, Arthur D., 158

M

Market condition analysis, 174–175
Market entry strategy, 34, 117
Marketing strategy, 85
Martin, Roger, 179
Maslow, Abraham, 66
McKinsey's three horizons of growth,
    56–60
  brief history, 56
  context and scenario to use, 57–58
  current and future, 57
  how to use, 58–60
Merger and acquisition (M&A)
    activities, 4, 108
Mintzberg, Henry, 183
Mission-driven culture, 93
Mobility barriers, 115

N

Nalebuff, Barry J., 124
National economic policy
    formulation, 141

O

Oberholzer-Gee, Felix, 88
Ohmae, Kenicki, 187
Osterwalder, Alexander, 71

P

Pareto Analysis, 48–52
  brief history, 48–49
  context and scenario to use, 49–50

evolution of, 49
    how to use, 51
Pareto, Vilfredo, 48
PESTEL, 137–140
    brief history, 137
    context and scenarios of use,
        138–139
    external business environment, 138
    how to use, 139–140
Pigneur, Yves, 71
Porter, Michael, 6, 106, 140, 191
Pre-emptive strike, 178
Pricing strategy, 34
Product development, 34, 86
Product life cycle management, 34
Product life cycle stages, 41–45
    brief history, 41
    context and scenario to use,
        42–43
    evolution of, 42
    how to use, 43–45
Ps of Strategy, 183–187
    brief history, 183
    flexible strategy, 183–184
    how to use, 184–187
Purchase frequency, 87

R

RBV. See Resource-based view (RBV)
Red Queen Effect, 120–124
    brief history, 120–121
    competitive landscape, 121
    context and scenario to use,
        121–122
    how to use, 123–124
Reese, Simon, 75
Regional development strategies, 142
Resource and capability assessment,
    175–176
Resource-based view (RBV)
    brief history, 2–3
    context and scenario for use, 3–5
    how to use, 5–6
    valuable elements of your
        business, 3
Rule of Three and Four, 103–106
    brief history, 103

competitive stability in the market,
    103–104
context and scenario to use,
    104–105
how to use, 105–106

S

Segment–Target–Position (STP),
    80–83
    brief history, 80
    context and scenario of use, 81–82
    refine your customer offer, 80–81
    how to use, 82–83
Senior, John, 67
Signaling defense, 178
Smith, Alan, 71
Smith, Wendell, 80
SOAR analysis
    brief history, 26
    broadening your business
        alignment, 26–27
    context and scenario for use, 27–28
    how to use, 28–30
SPACE Analysis, 168–173
    brief history, 168
    create a consolidated strategy, 169
    how to use, 169–173
Still factual and controllable
    BCG growth-share matrix, 52–56
    break-even analysis, 45–48
    characteristic checklist, 60
    characteristics band, 31–32
    diffusion of innovation, 37–41
    Kotler's 5 product levels, 33–36
    McKinsey's three horizons of
        growth, 56–60
    Pareto analysis, 48–52
    product life cycle stages, 41–45
STP. See Segment–Target–Position
    (STP)
Strategic flexibility, 176–177
Strategic Group Analysis, 115–120
    brief history, 115
    competitors in industry, 116
    context and scenario to use,
        116–118
    how to use, 118–120

Strategic planning, 142
Strategy Diamond, 196–200
   brief history, 196
   strategy with competitive
      advantage, 196
   how to use, 196–200
SWOT analysis
   Brief History, 19
   Context and Scenario for Use,
      20–21
   Internal and External
      Perspectives, 19
   How to Use, 21–22

T

Tangible resources, 5
3 Cs Model, 187–191
   brief history, 187
   comprehensive strategy, 188
   how to use, 188–191
TOWS analysis
   brief history, 22–23
   context and scenario for use, 23–24
   to strategy, 23
   how to use, 25–26

U

Ulwick, Anthony, 63
Undifferentiated circle, 177

V

Valen, Leigh Van, 120
Value Chain Analysis
   brief history, 6–7

   primary and secondary activities,
      7–9
   how to use, 9–10
Value Proposition Canvas, 71–75
   brief history, 71
   context and scenario to use, 72–73
   customer pains and gains to your
      offerings, 71
   how to use, 73–75
Value Stick, 88–94
   brief history, 88–89
   context and scenario to use, 89–90
   customer and collaborator
      checklist, 94–95
   how to use, 90–94
   value of your customers, 89
Vasconcellos e Sá, Jorge, 173
Vernon, Raymond, 41, 152
VRIO analysis
   brief history, 11
   competitive advantage, 12
   context and scenario for use, 12–13
   how to use, 14–15

W

Wernerfelt, Birger, 3
Willingness to pay (WTP), 88
Willingness to sell (WTS), 88
Withdrawal, 178
WTP. *See* Willingness to pay (WTP)
WTS. *See* Willingness to sell (WTS)

www.ingramcontent.com/pod-product-compliance
Lightning Source LLC
Chambersburg PA
CBHW061157220326
41599CB00025B/4512